THIS BOOK BELONGS TO

Check Out Other Books by Rae Maker

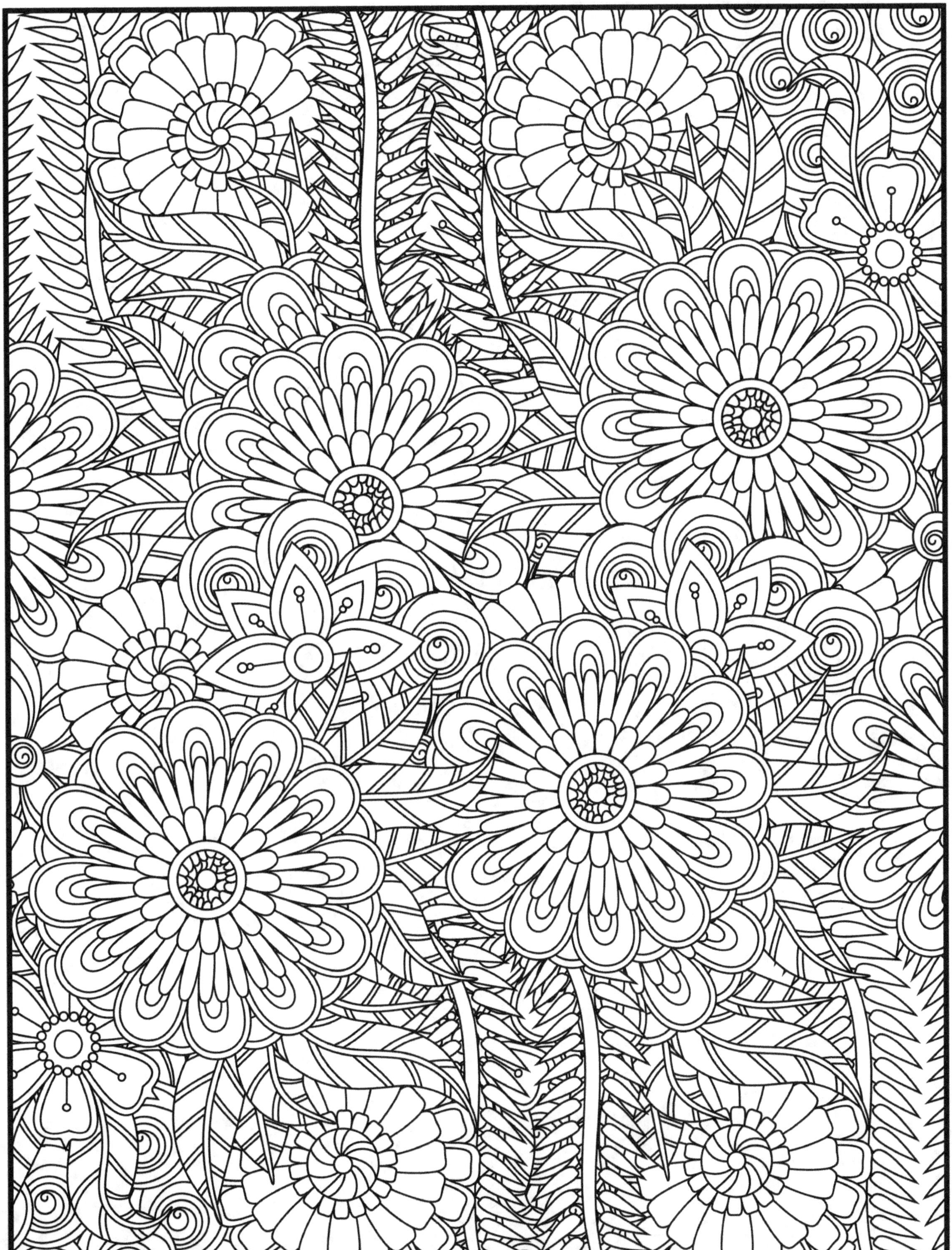

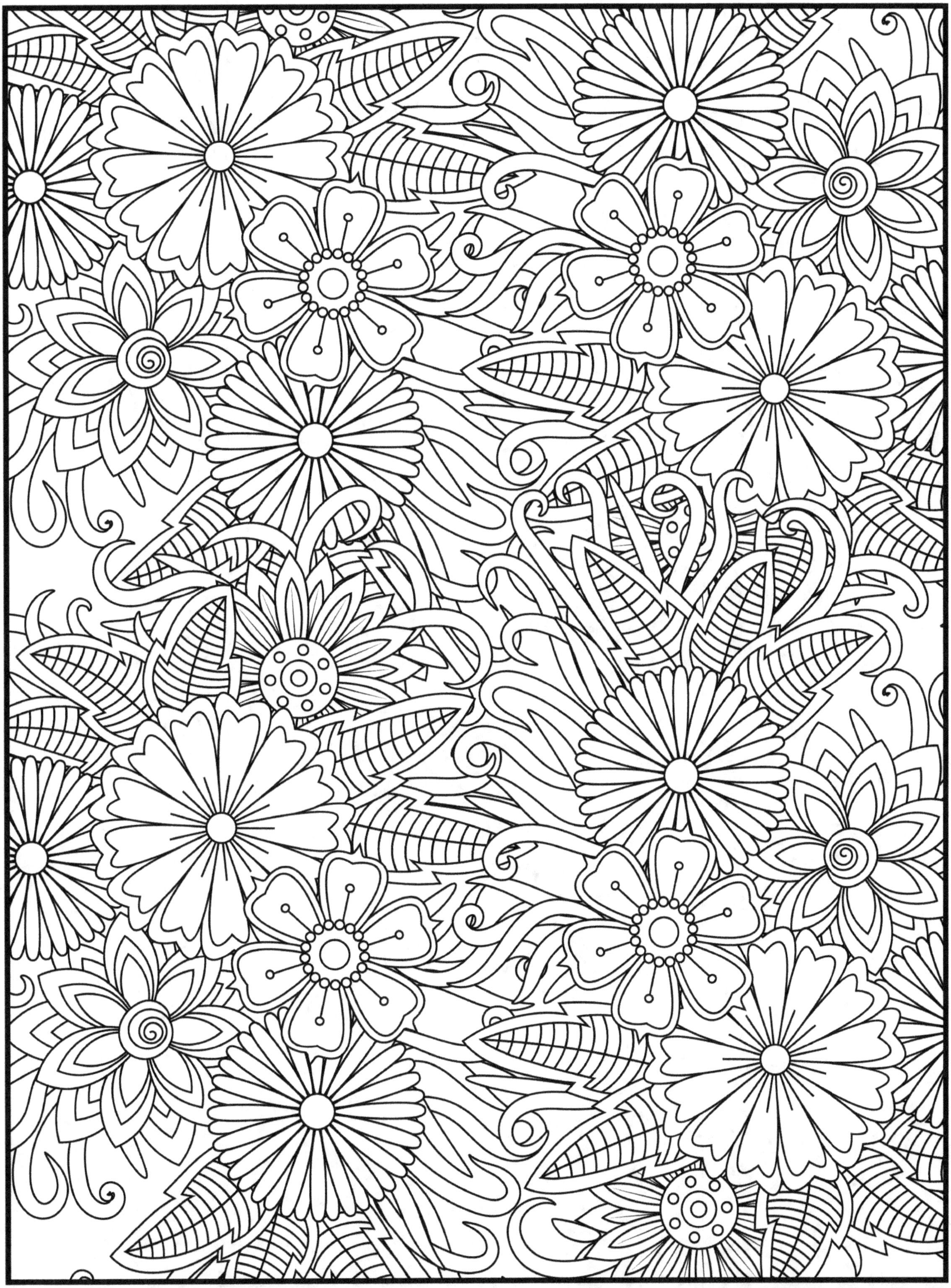

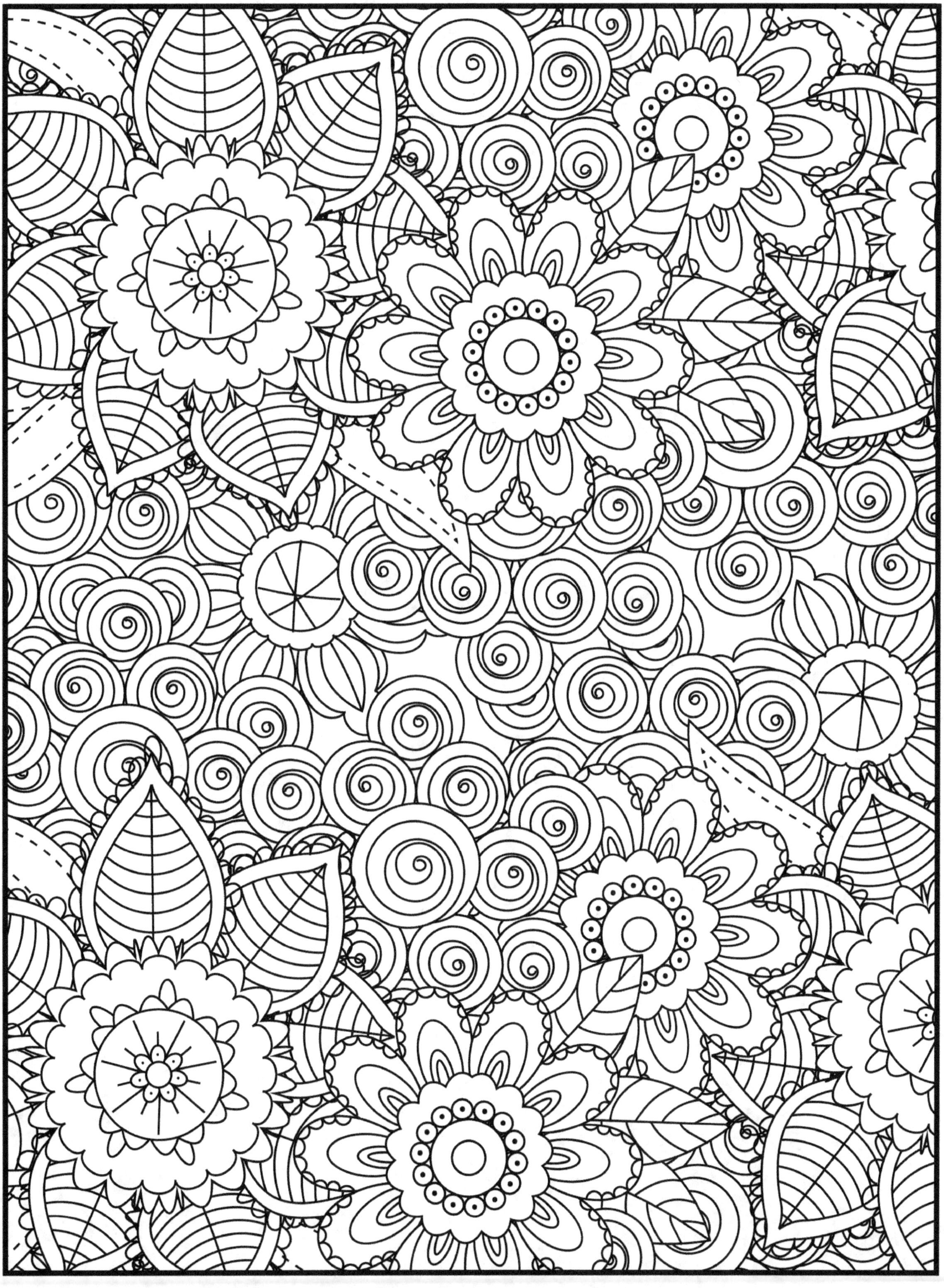

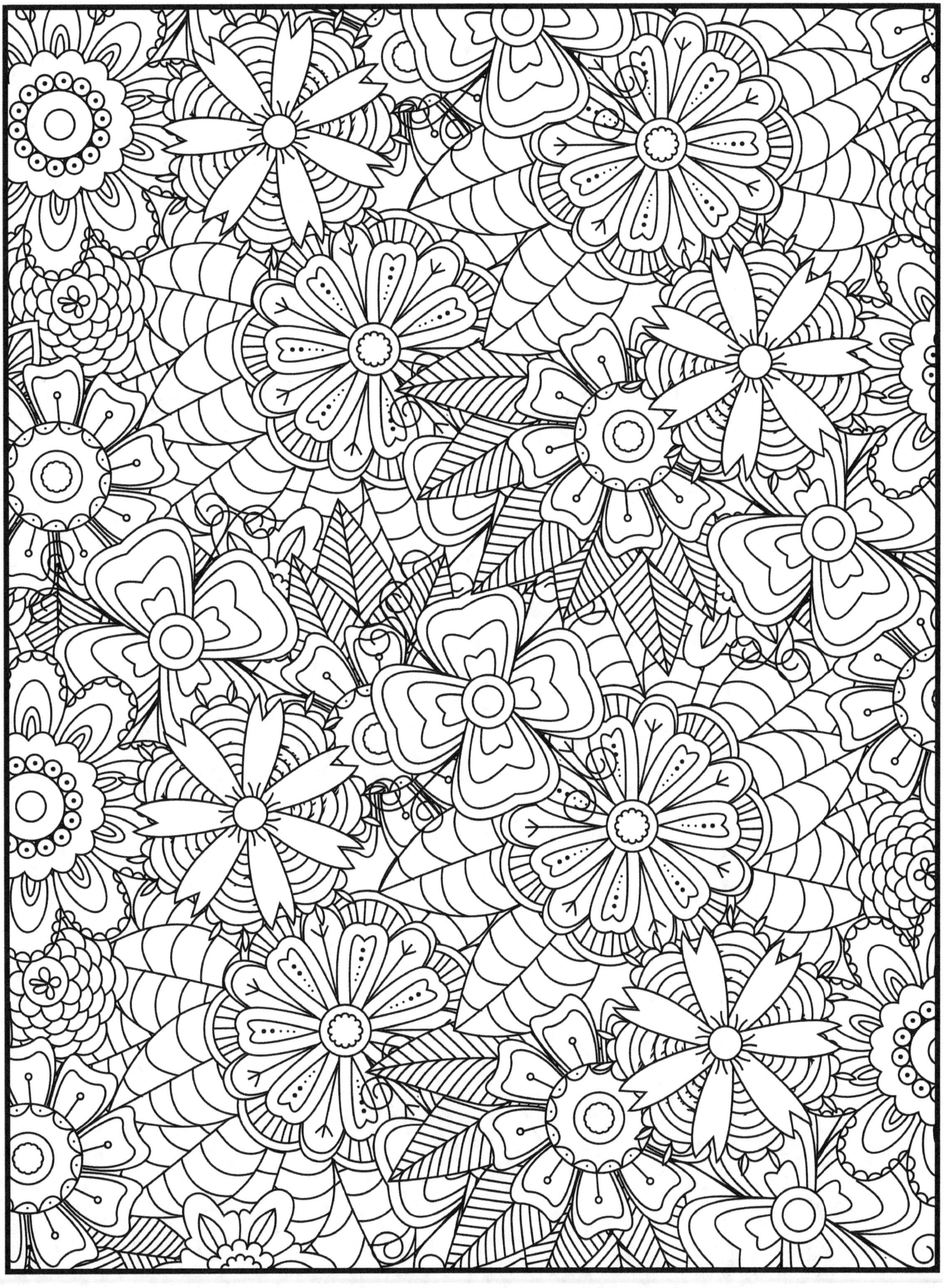

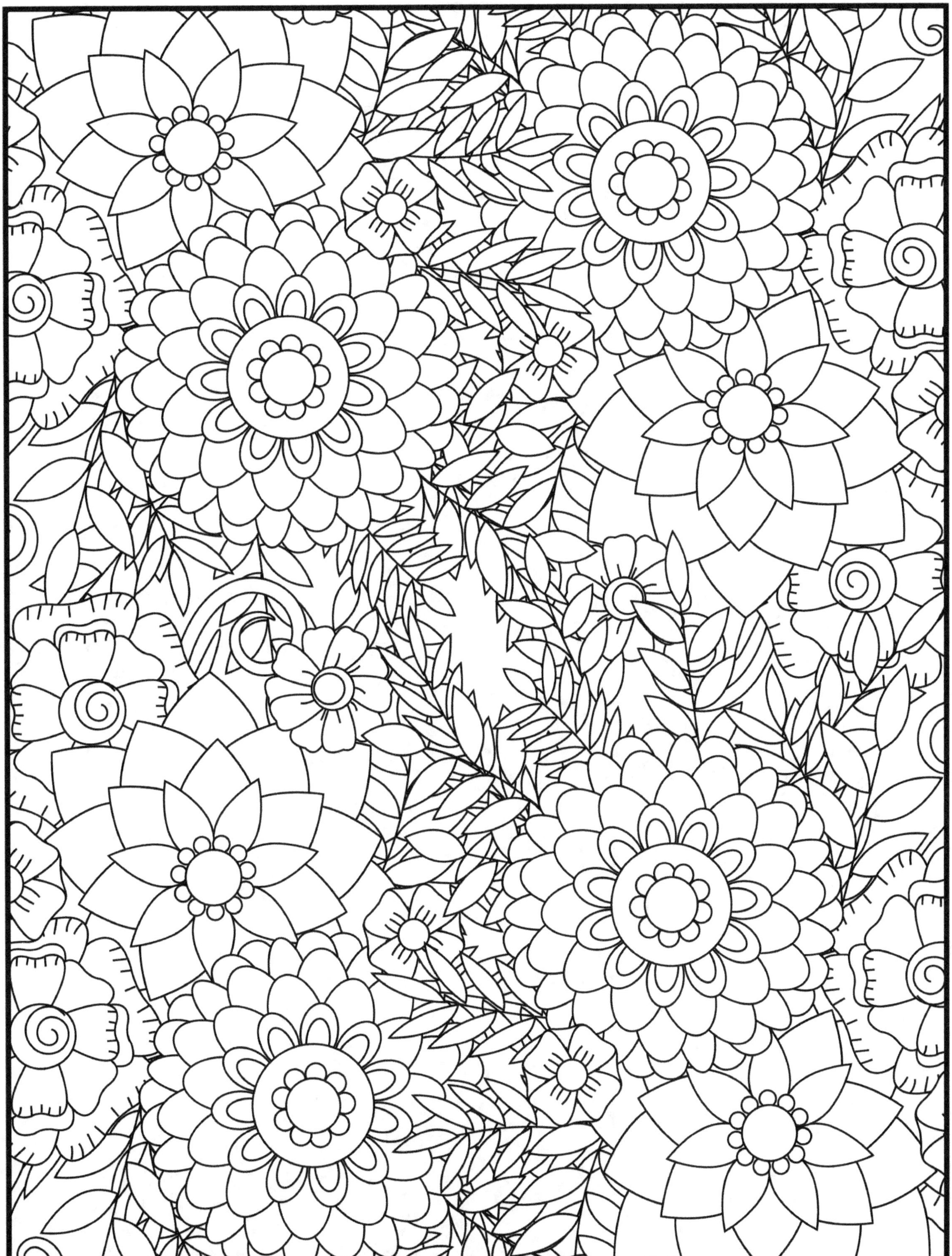

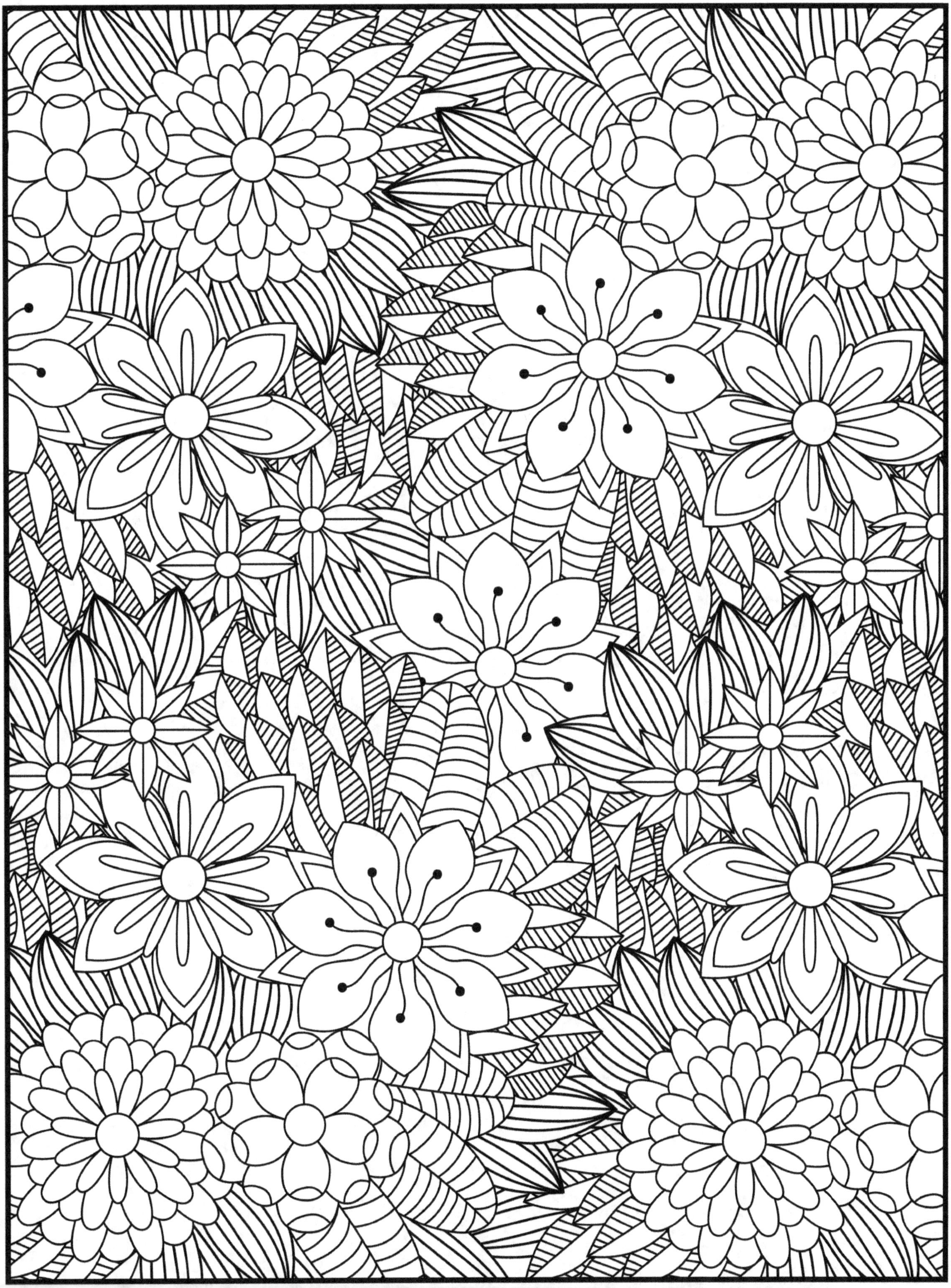

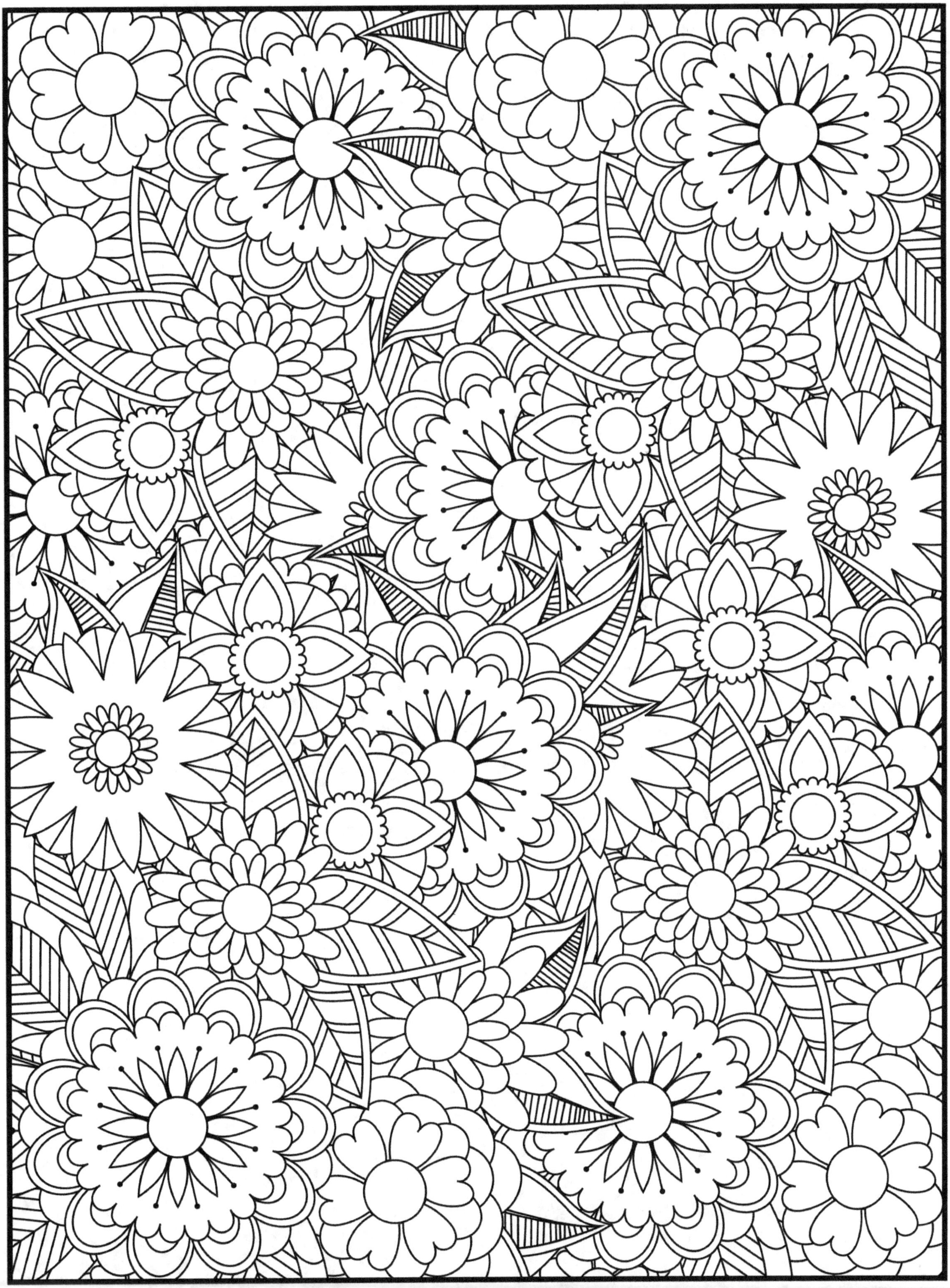

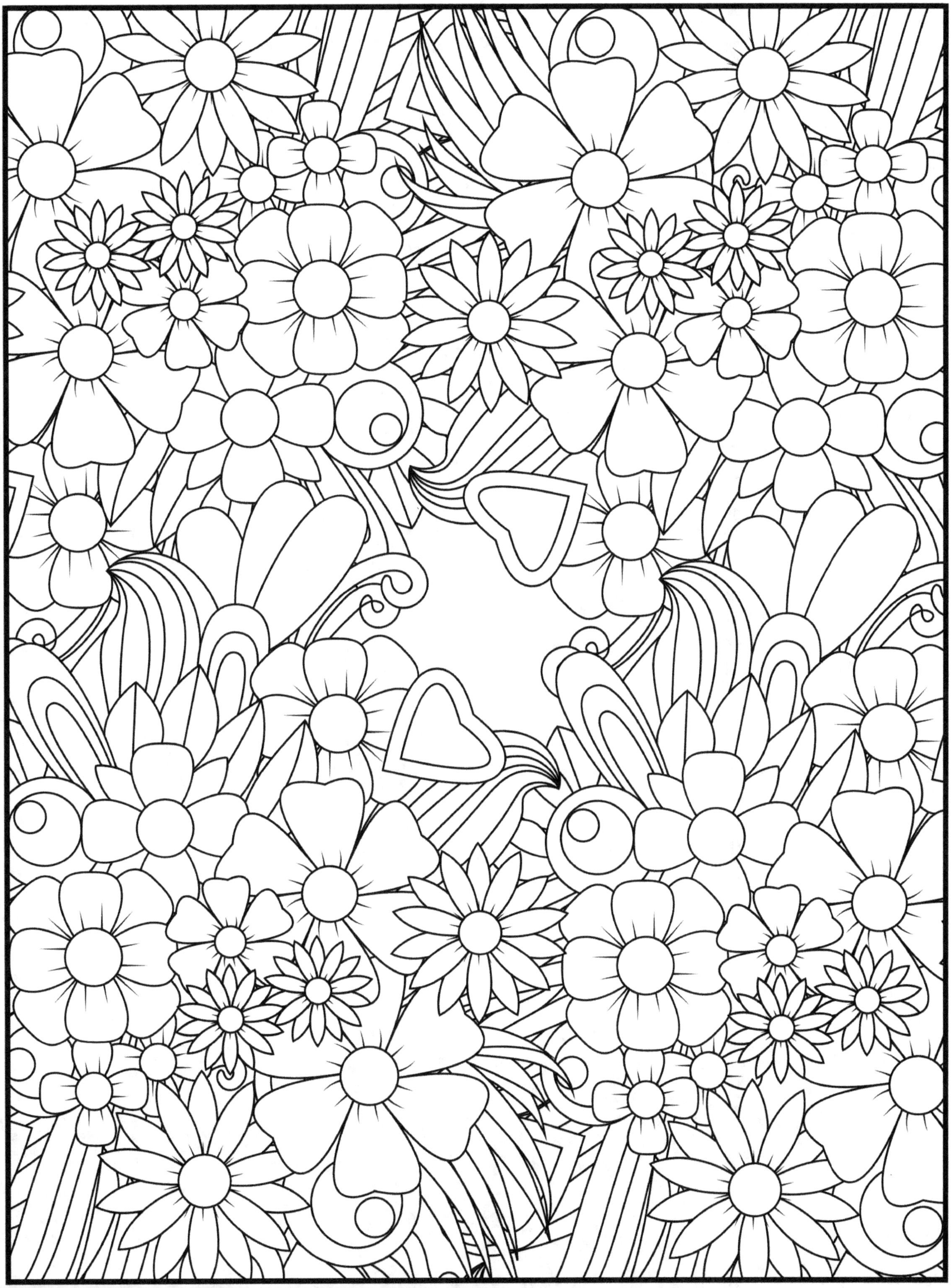

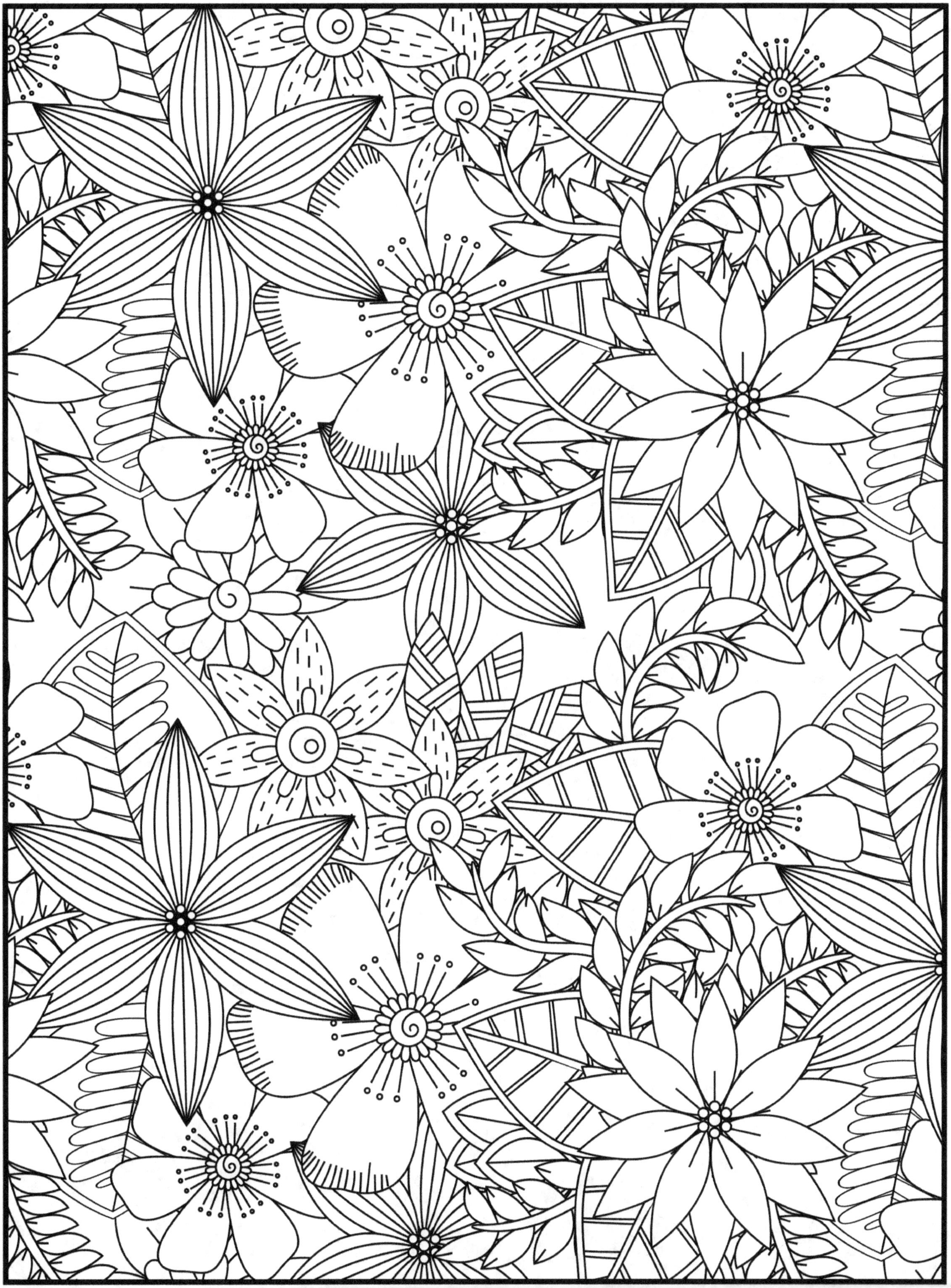

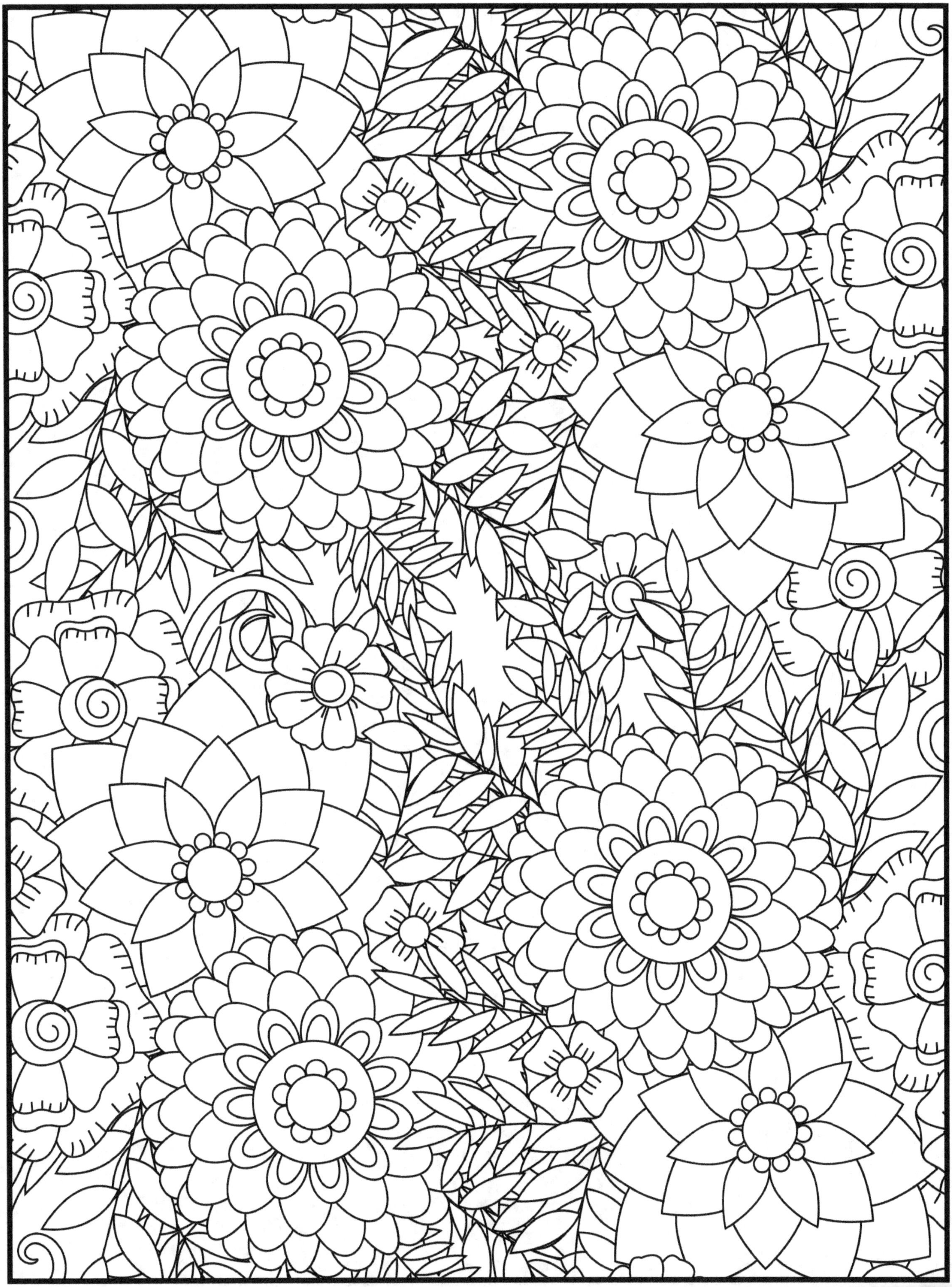

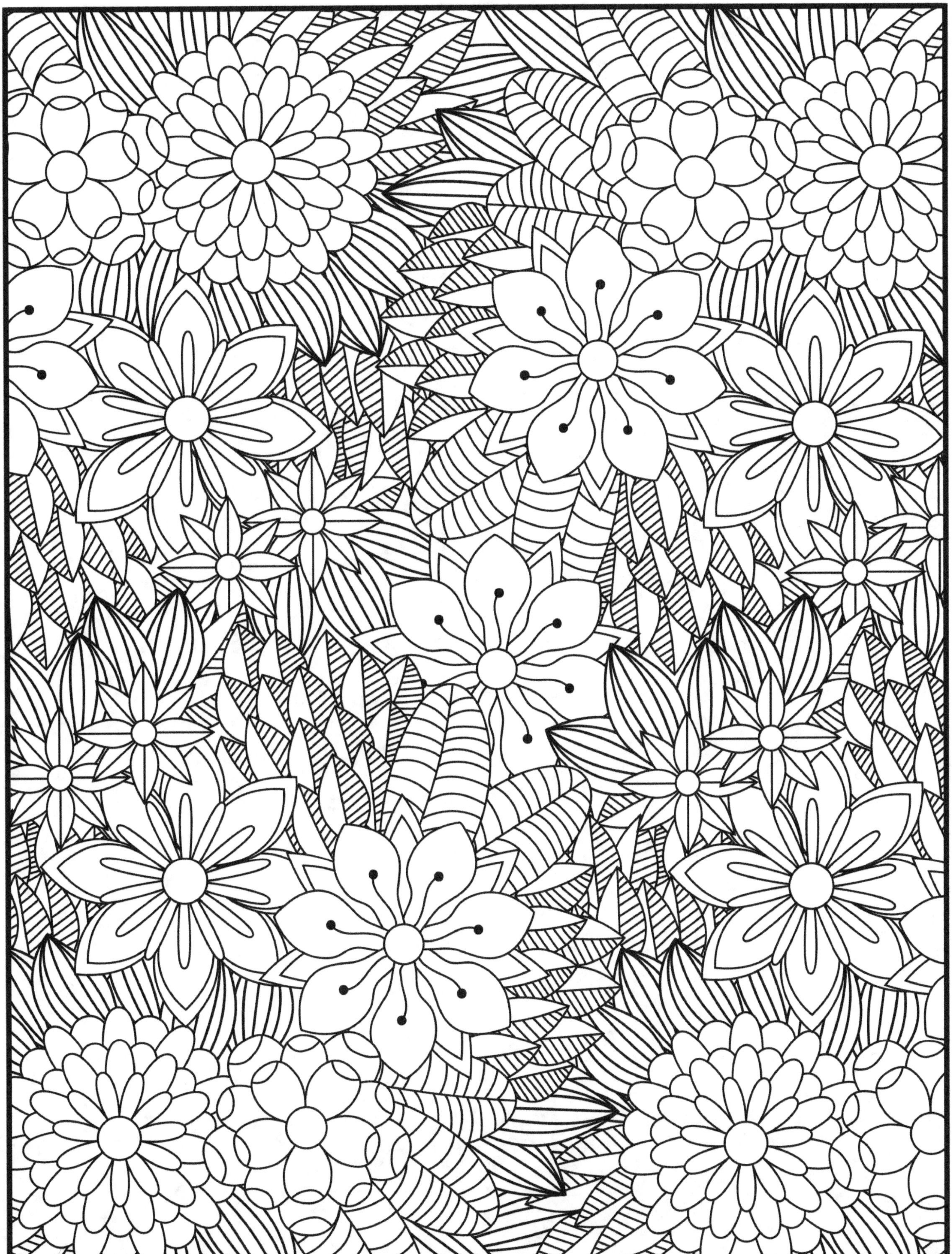

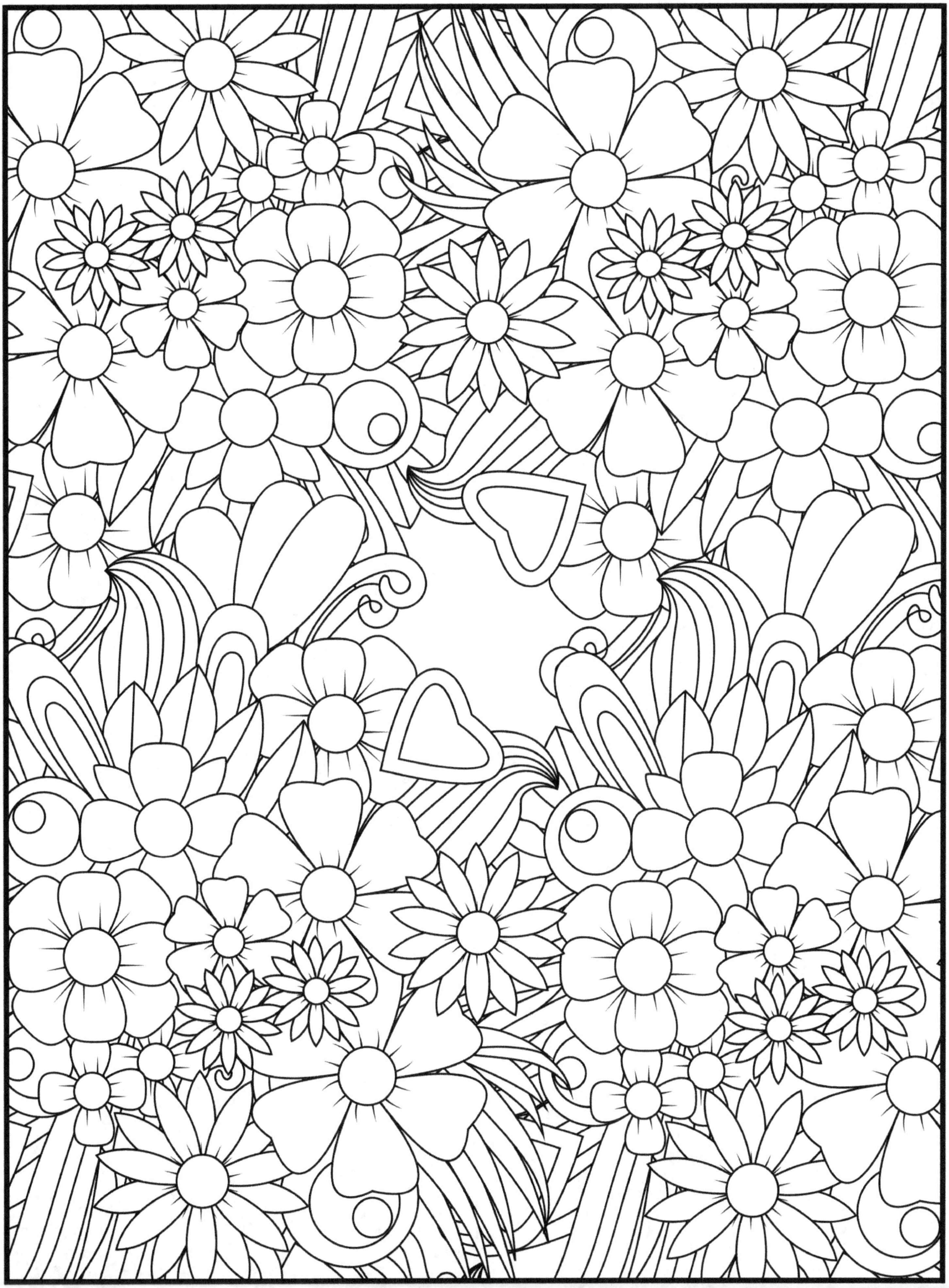

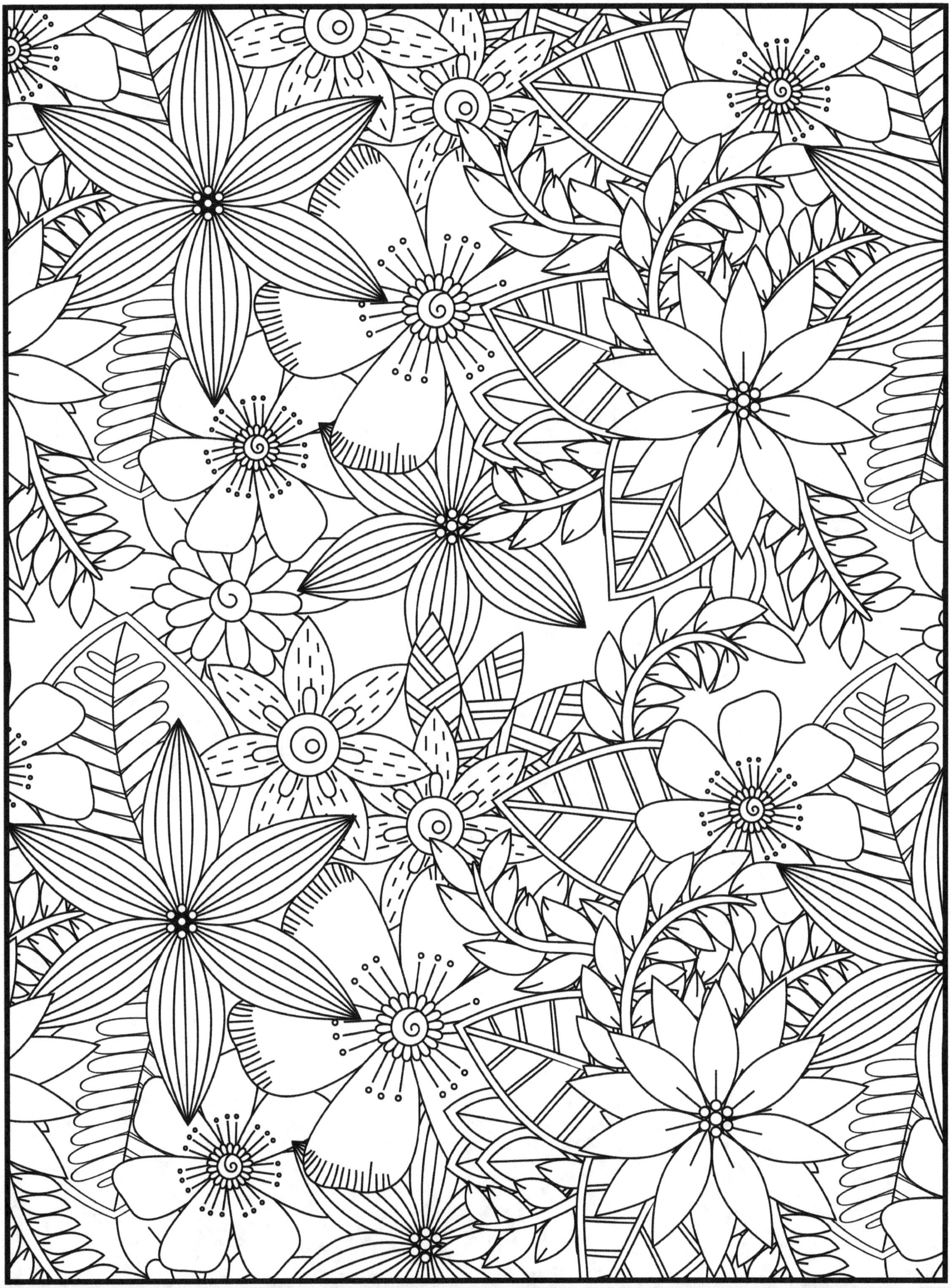

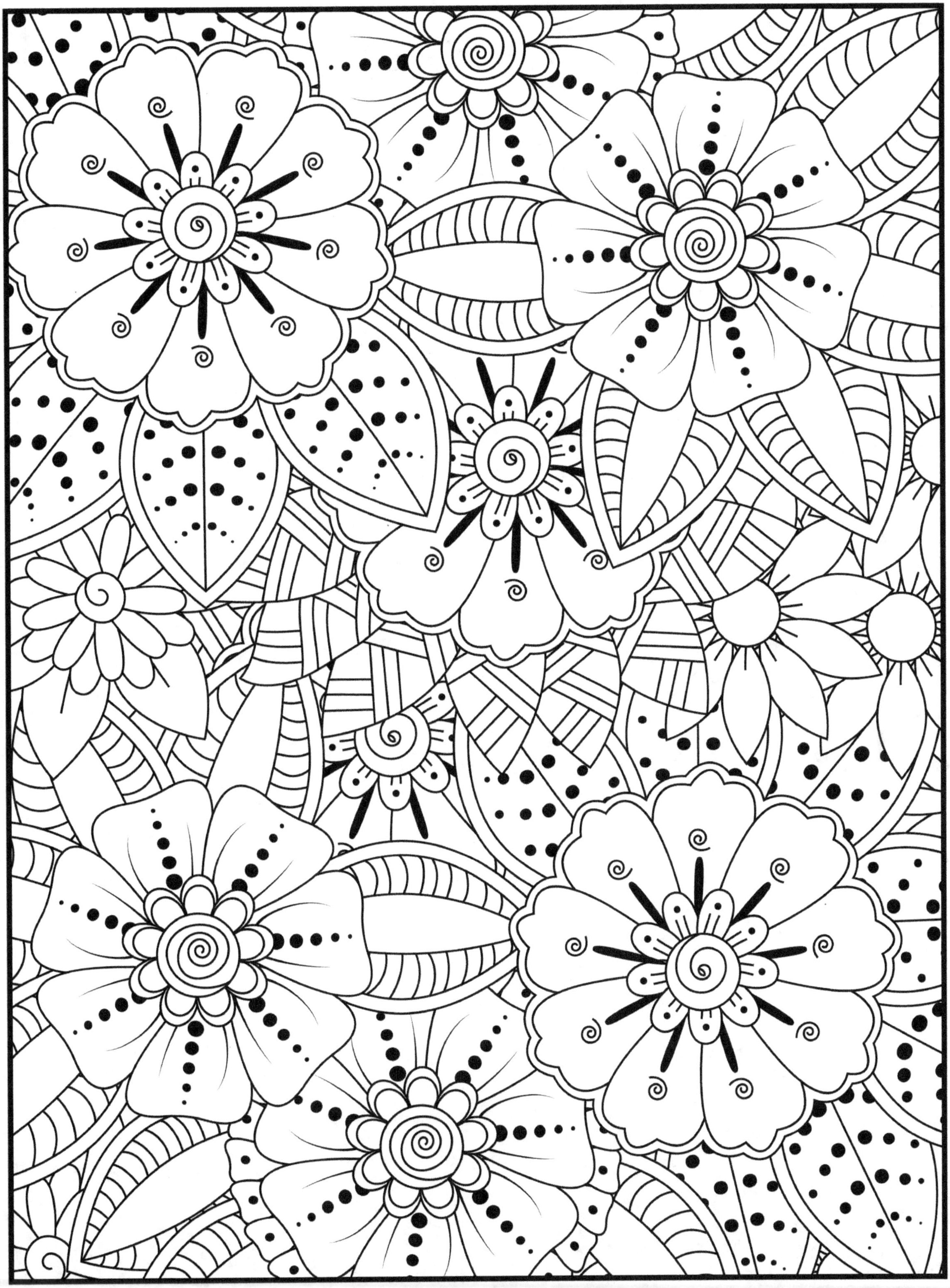

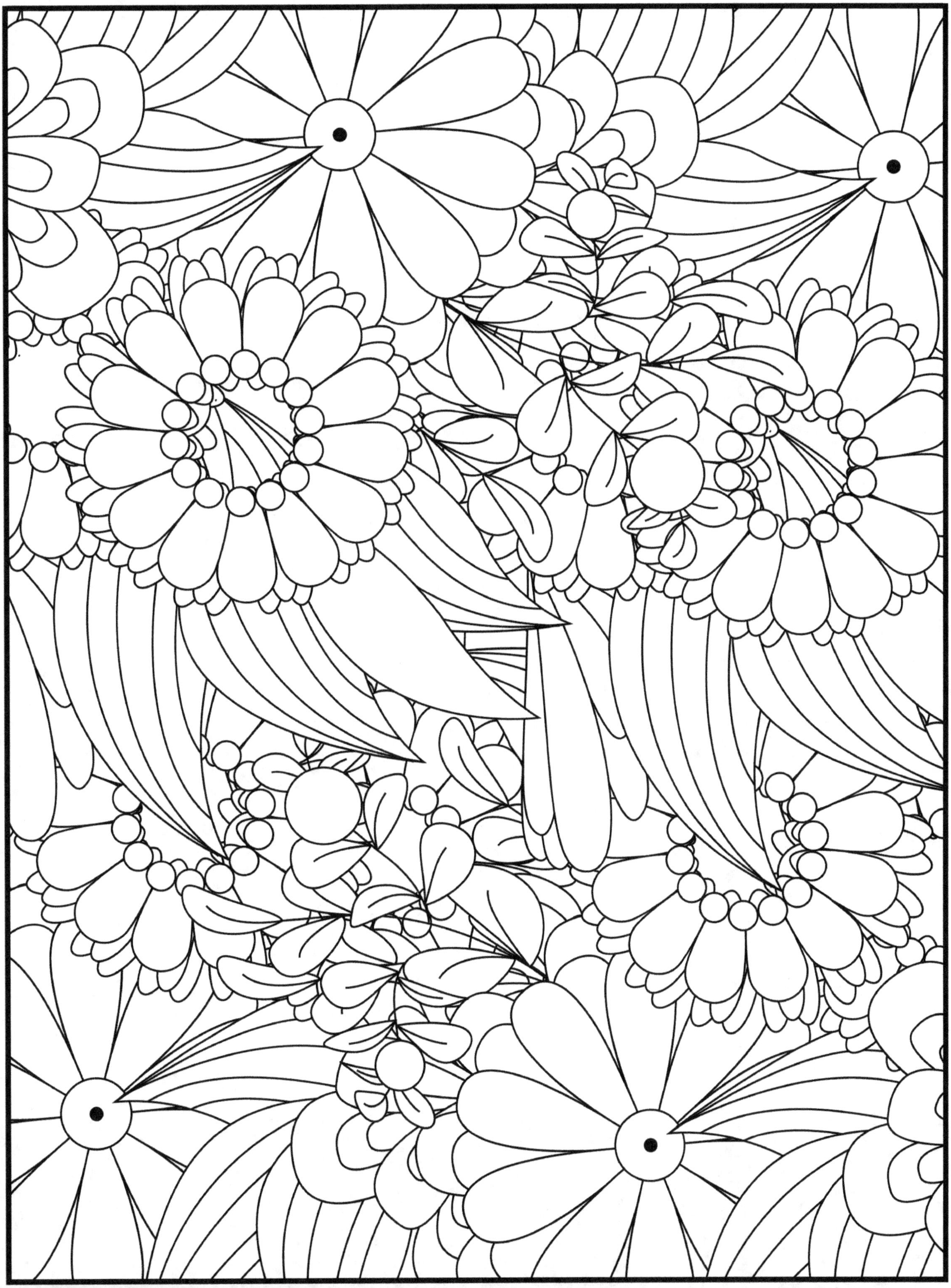

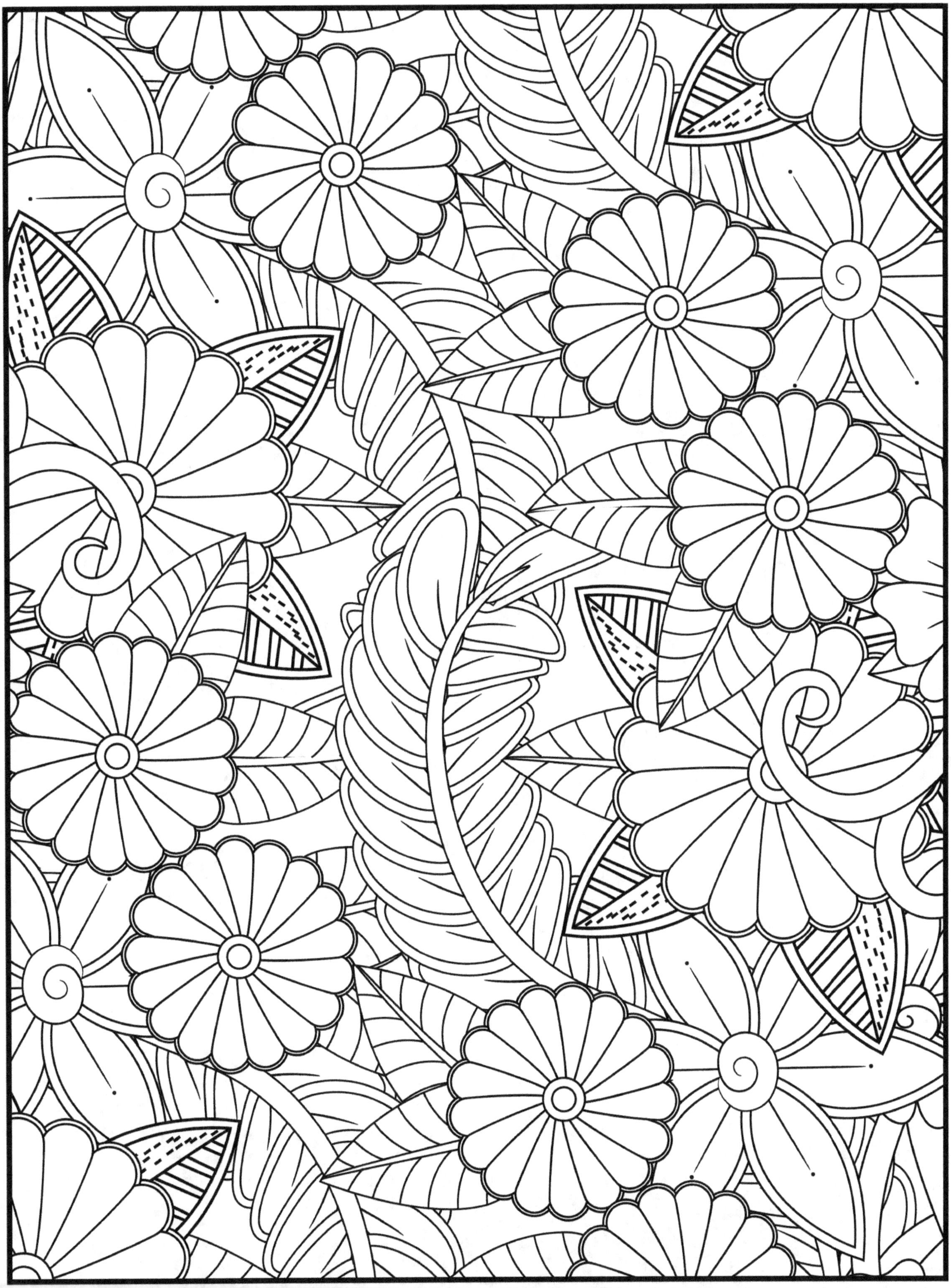

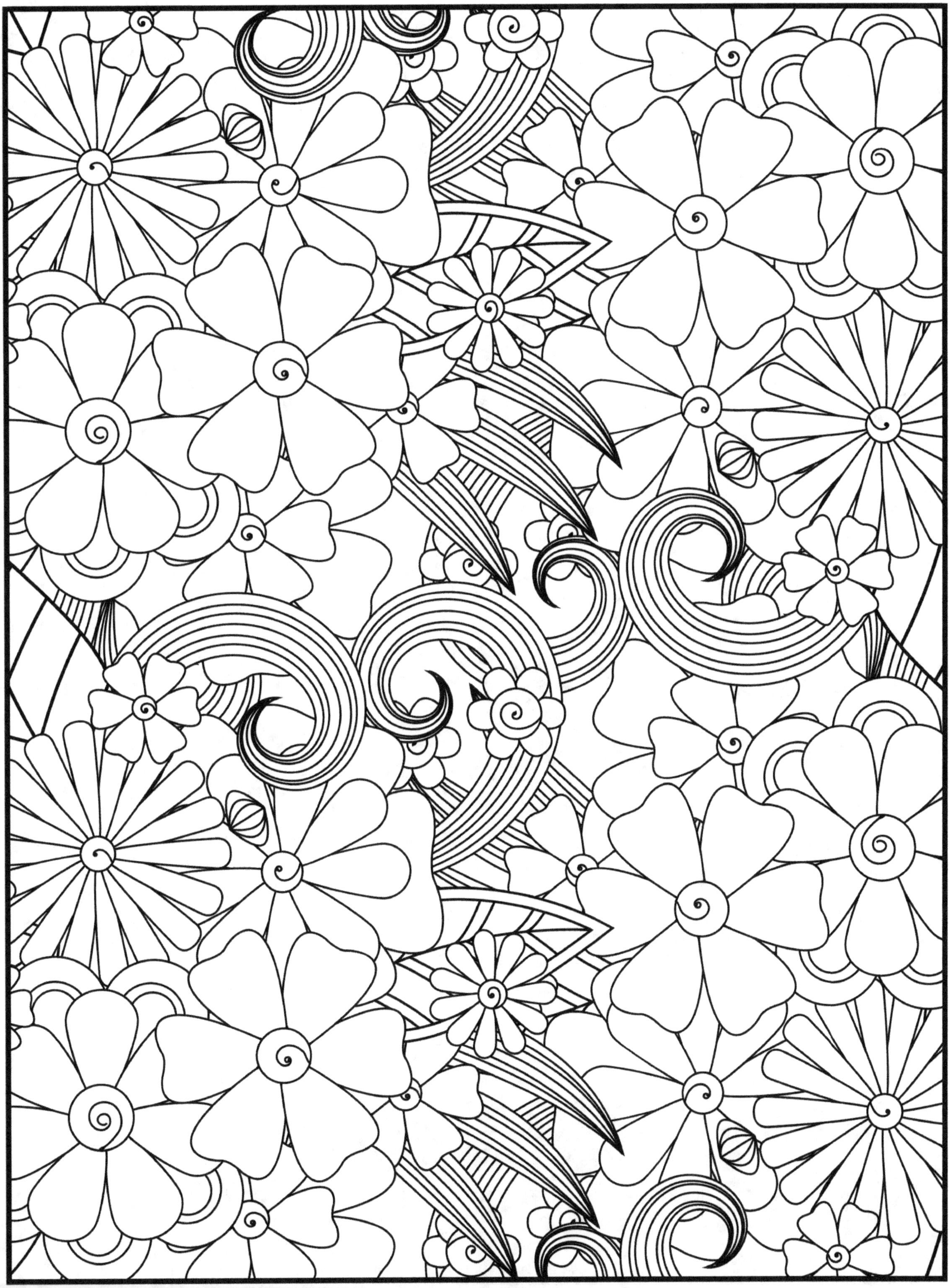

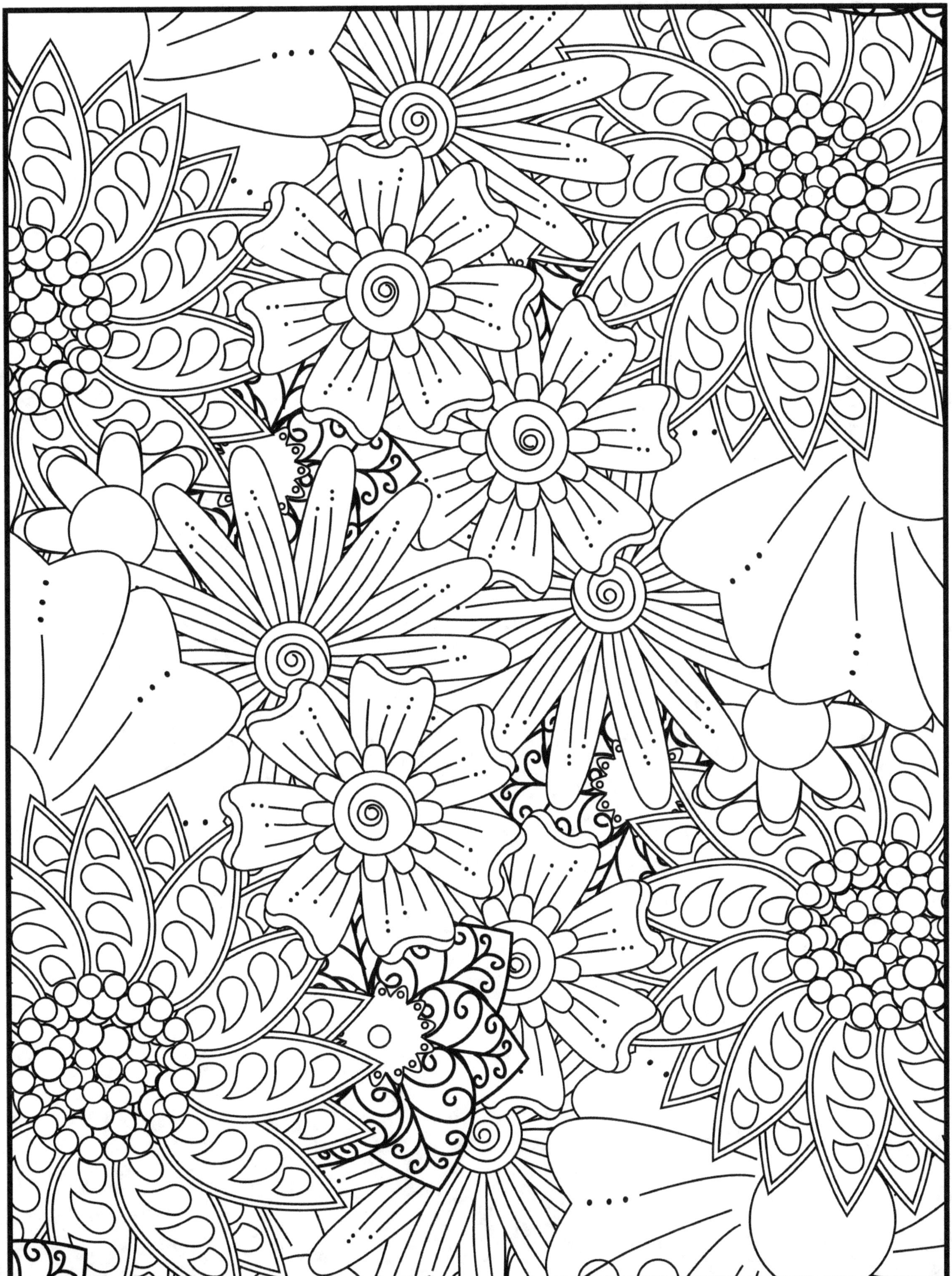

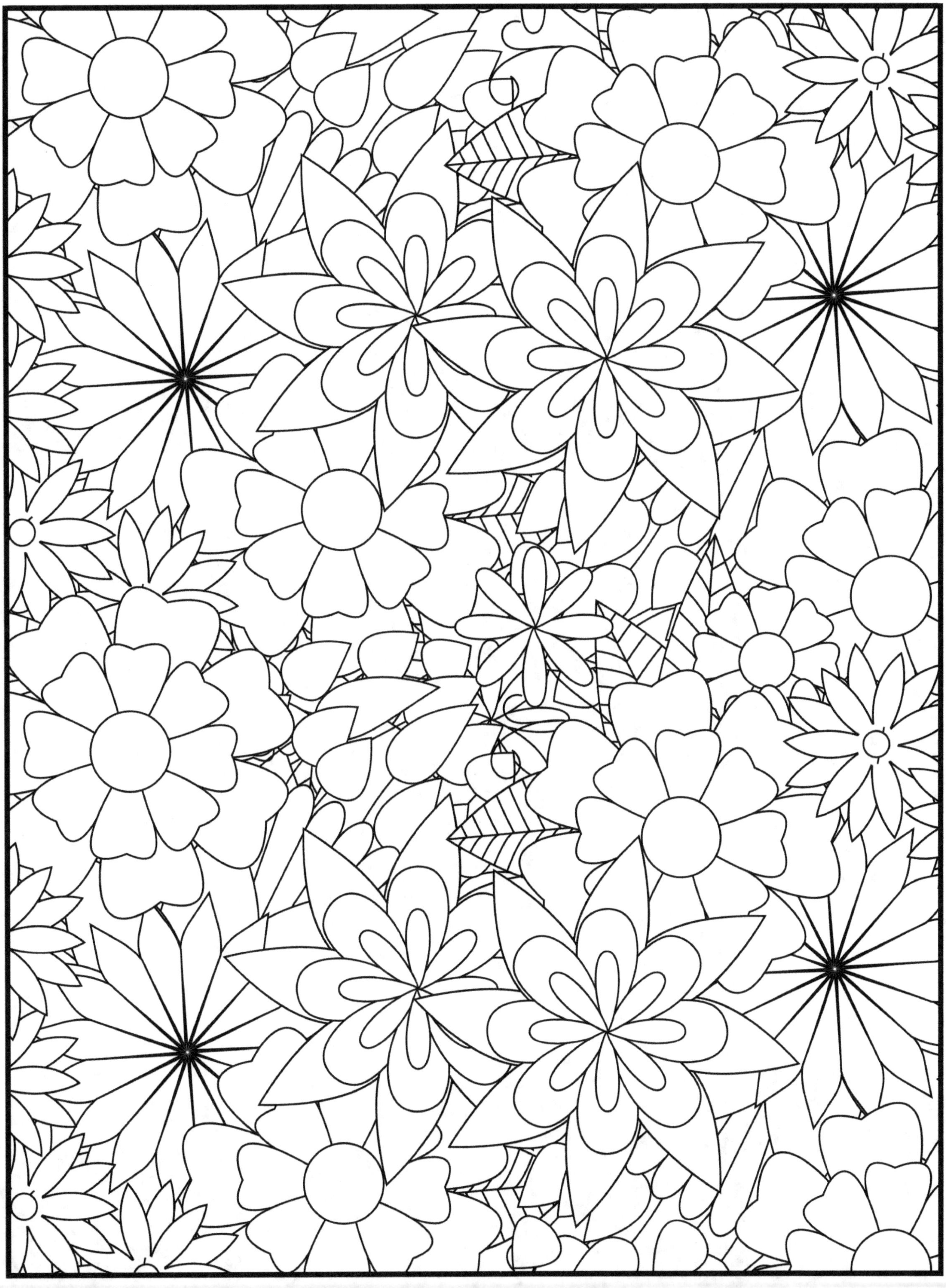

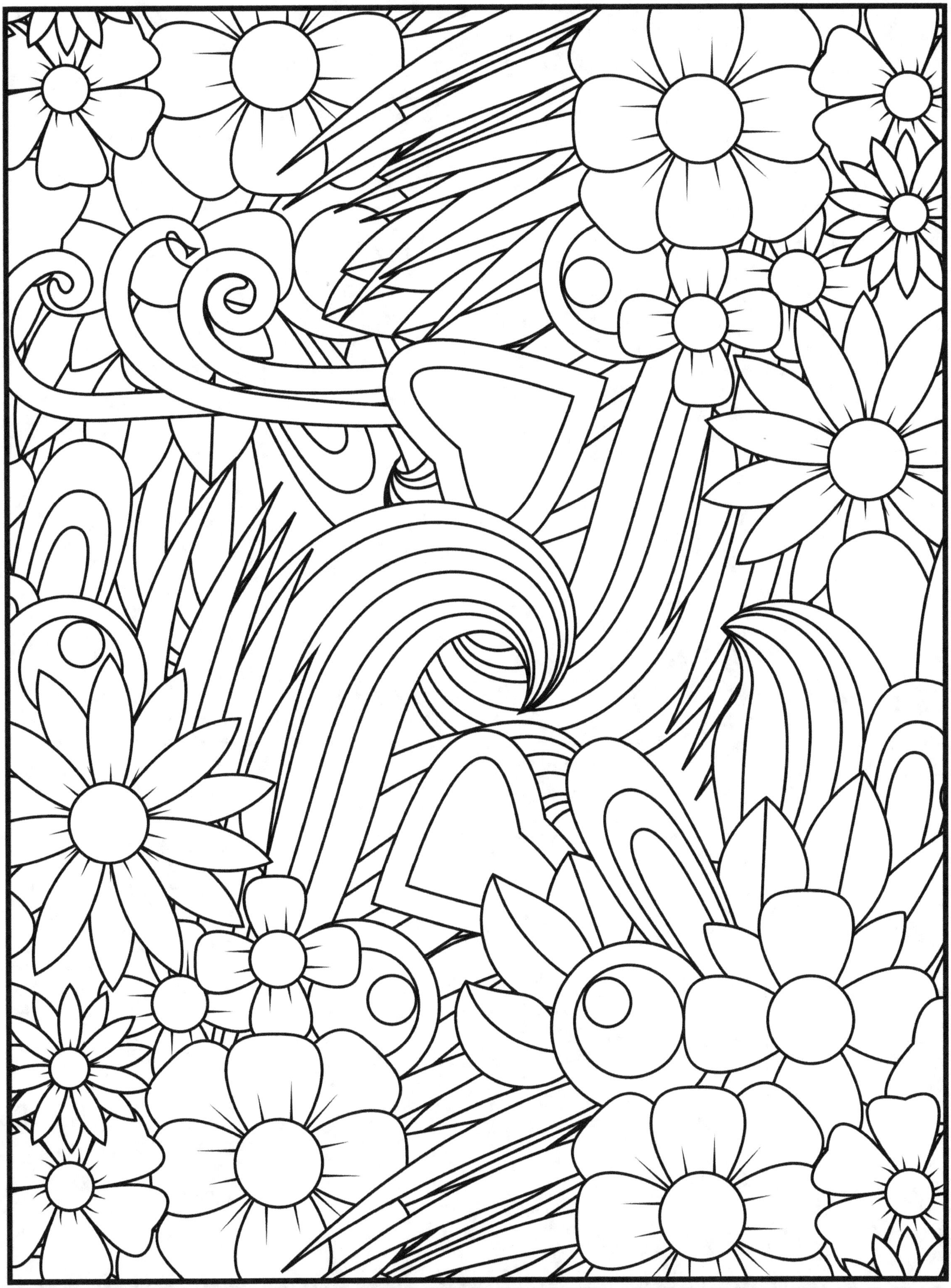

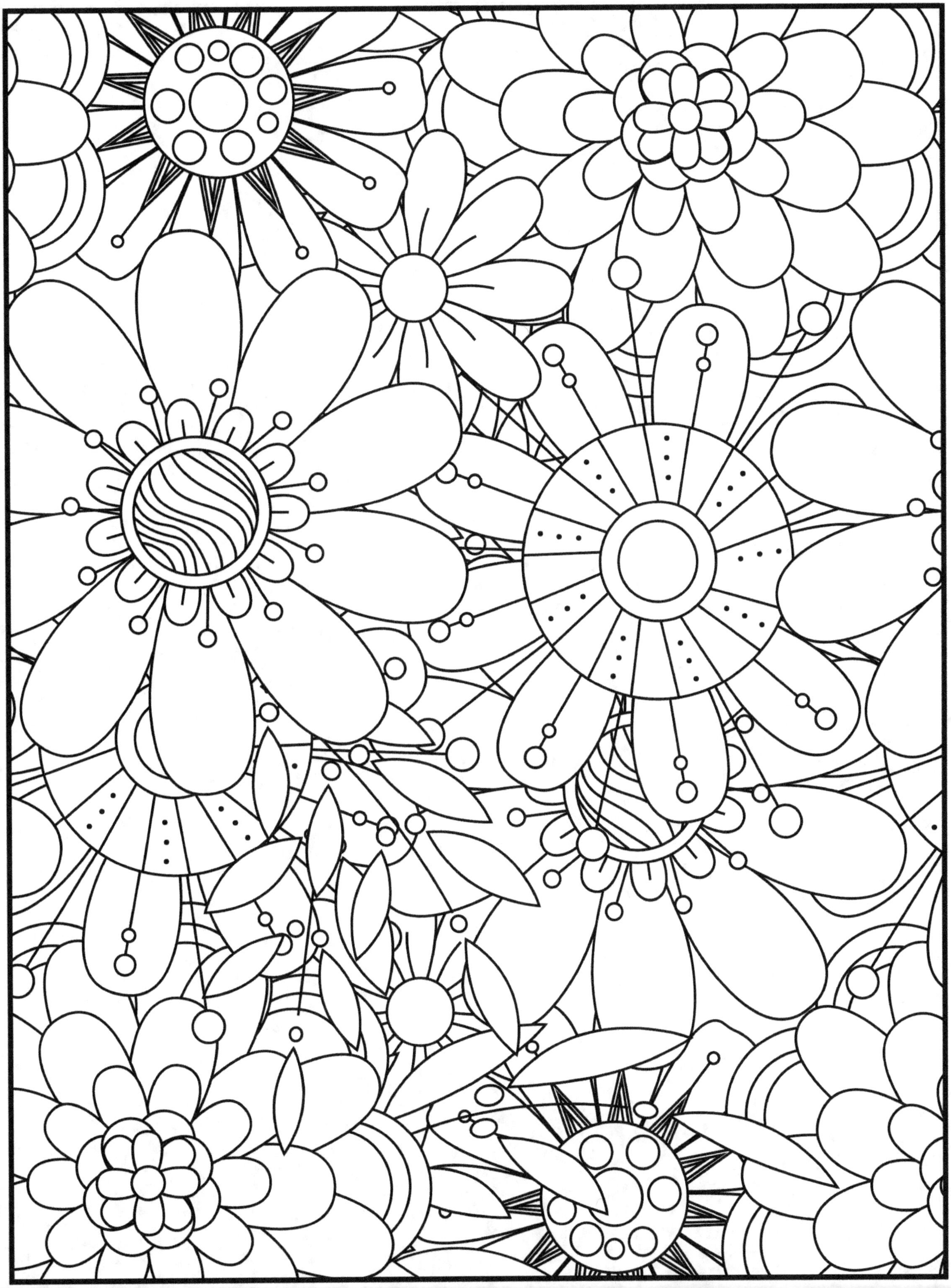

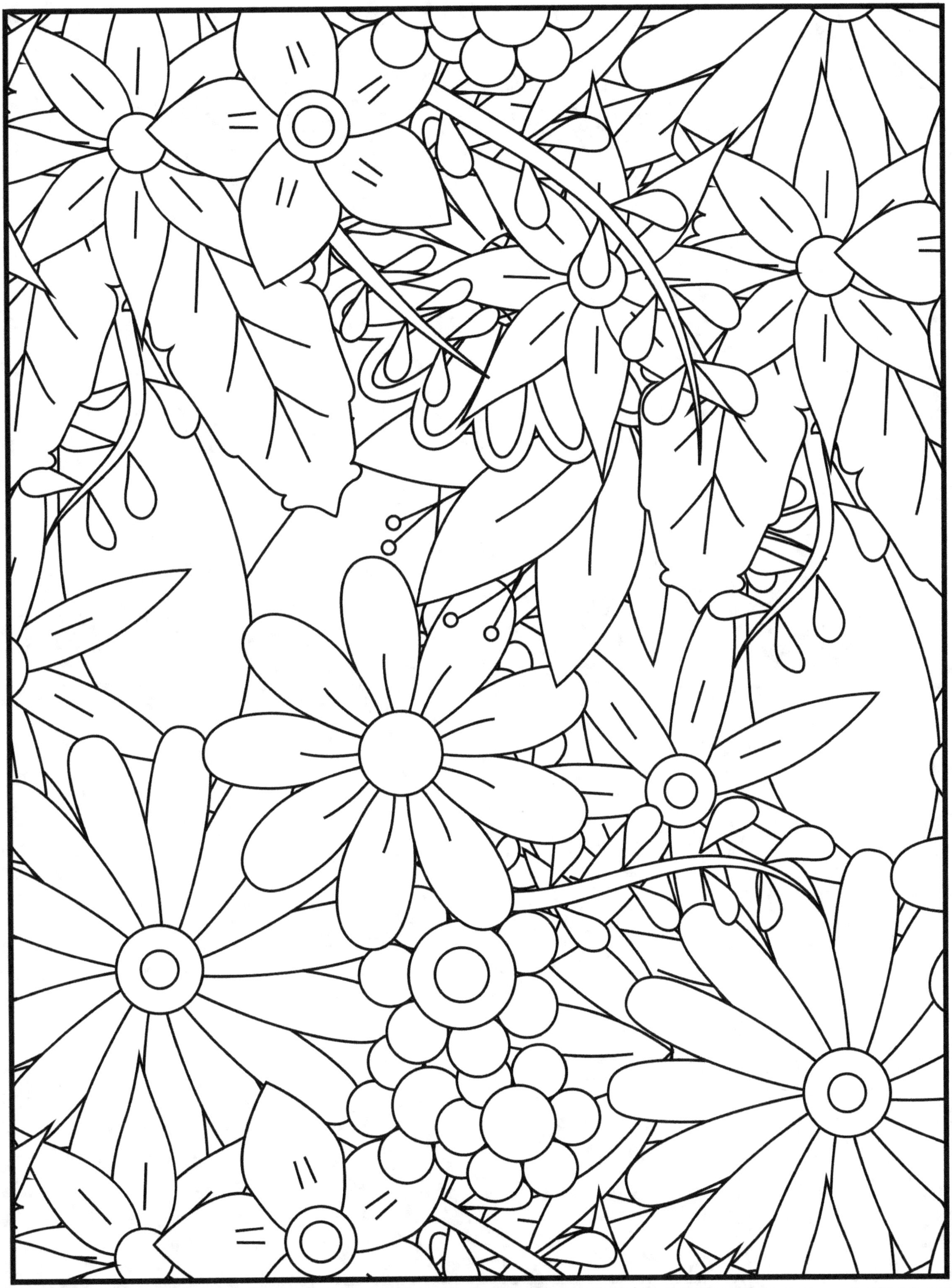

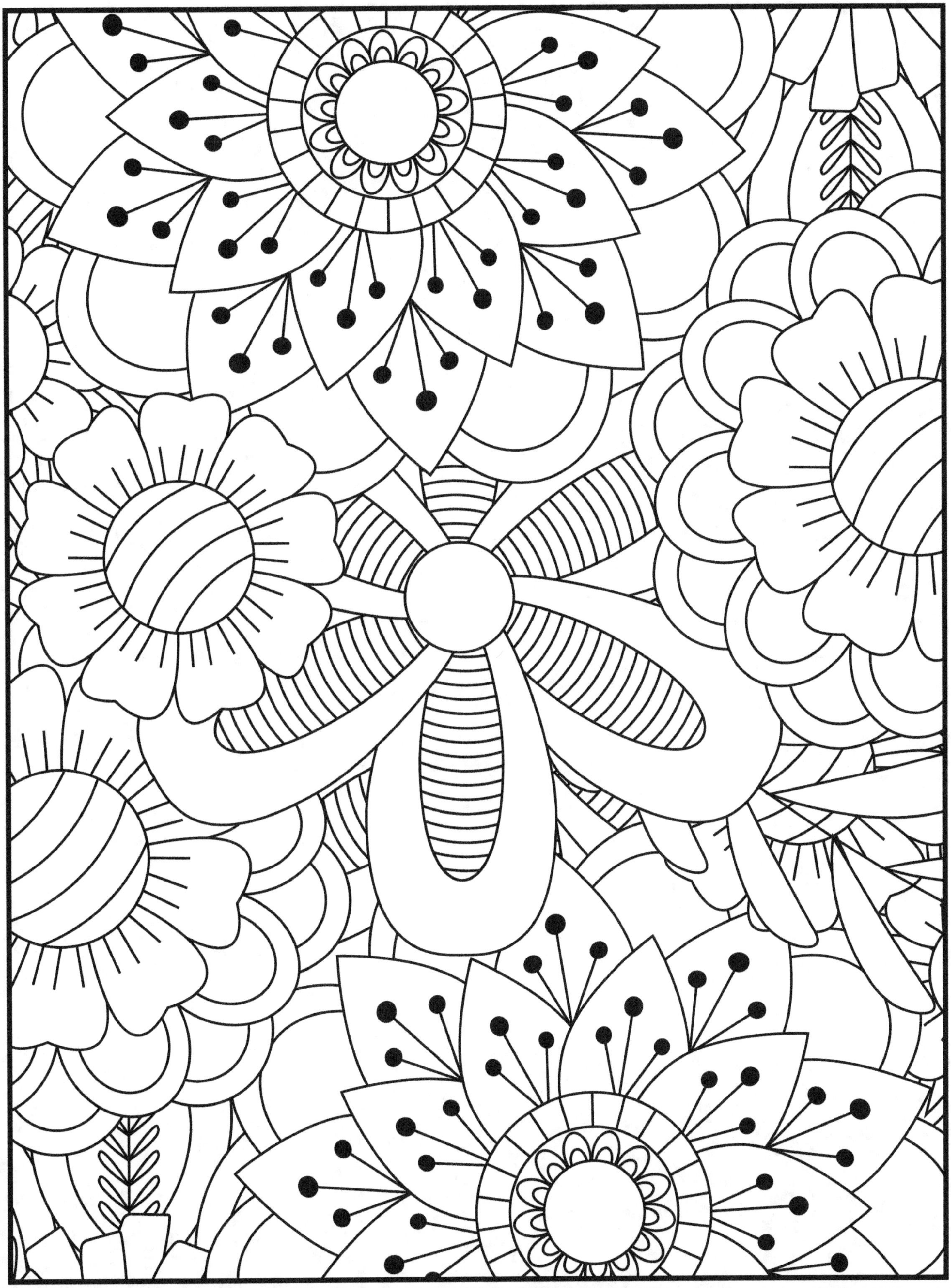

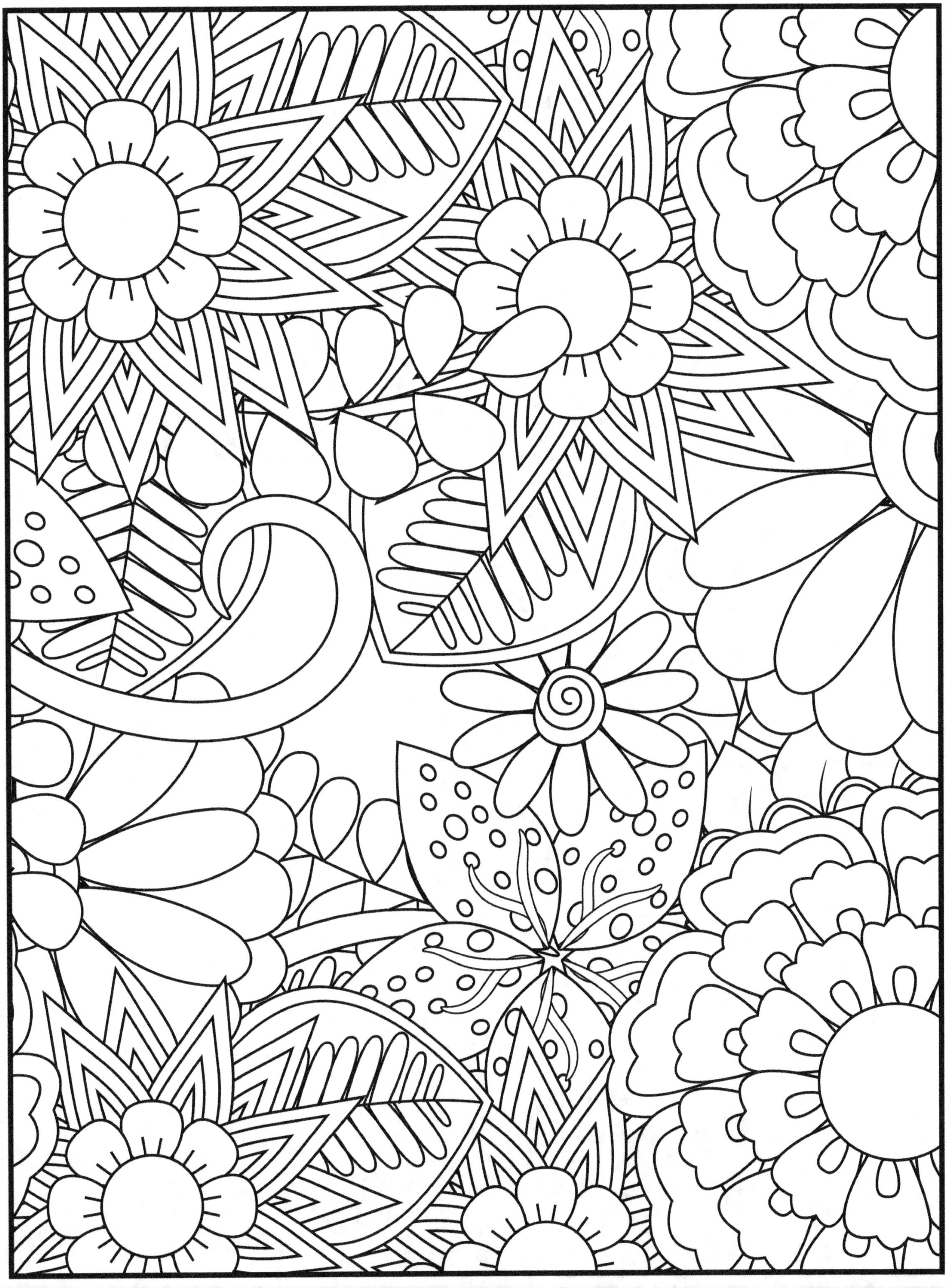

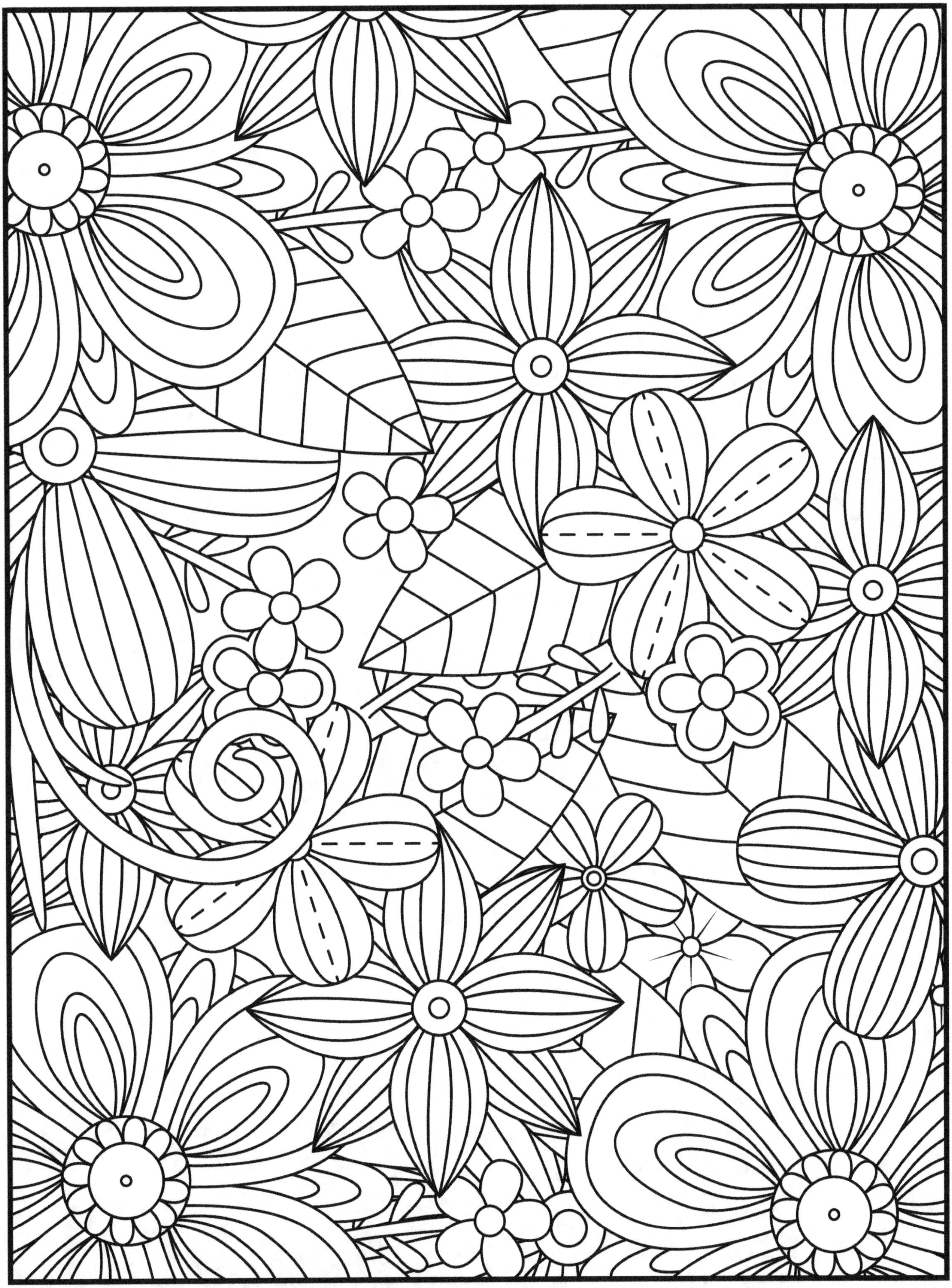

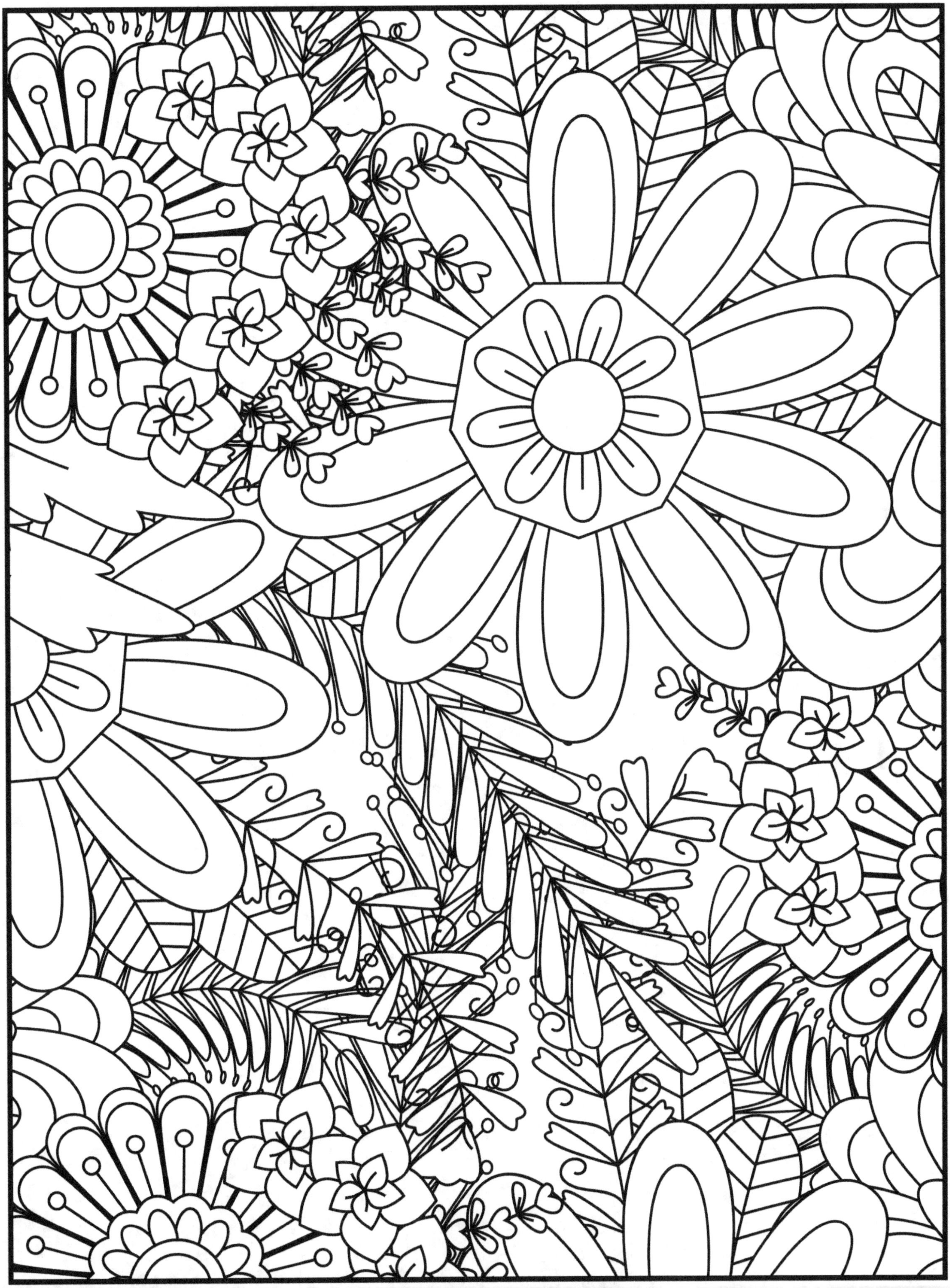

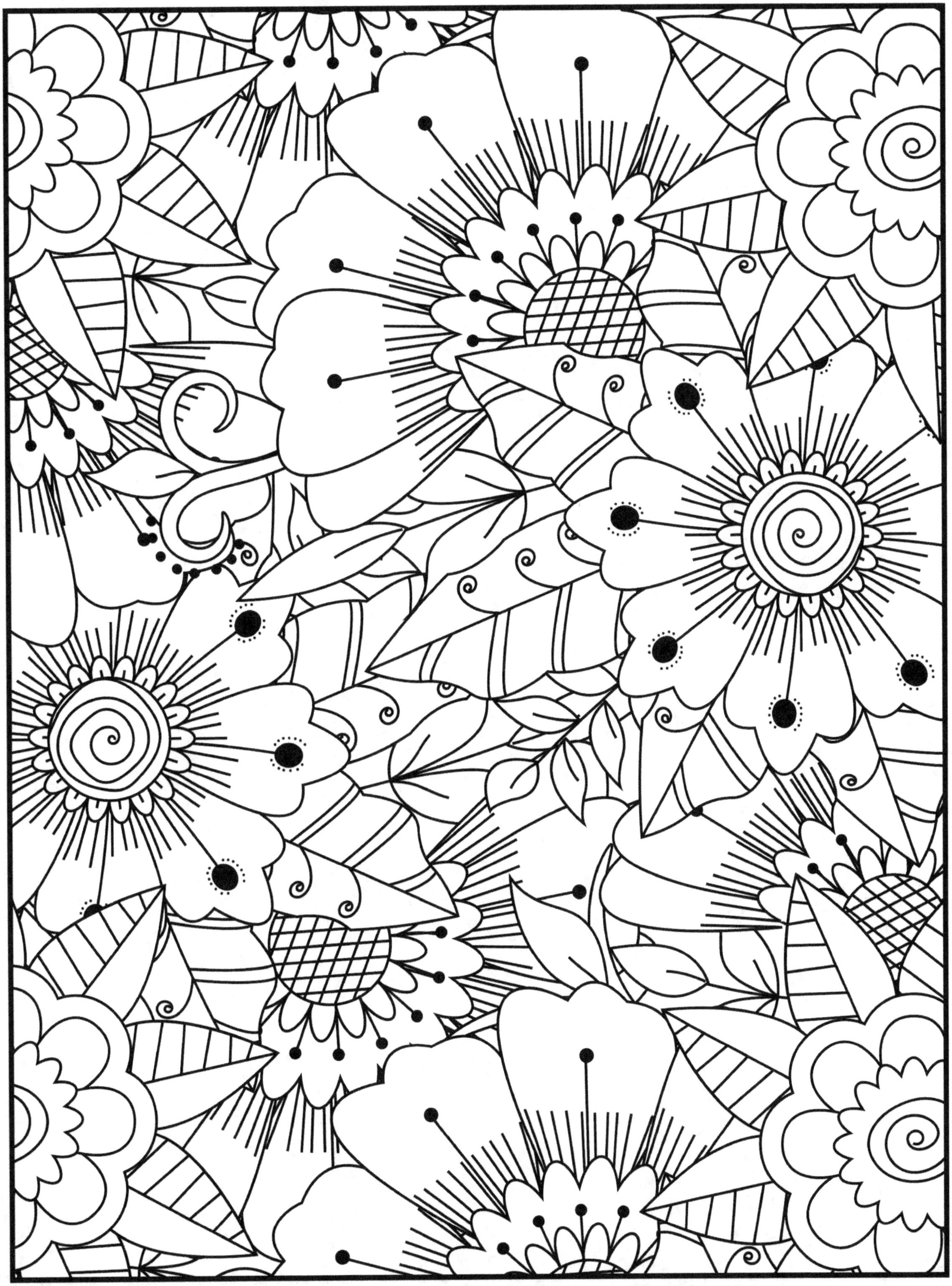

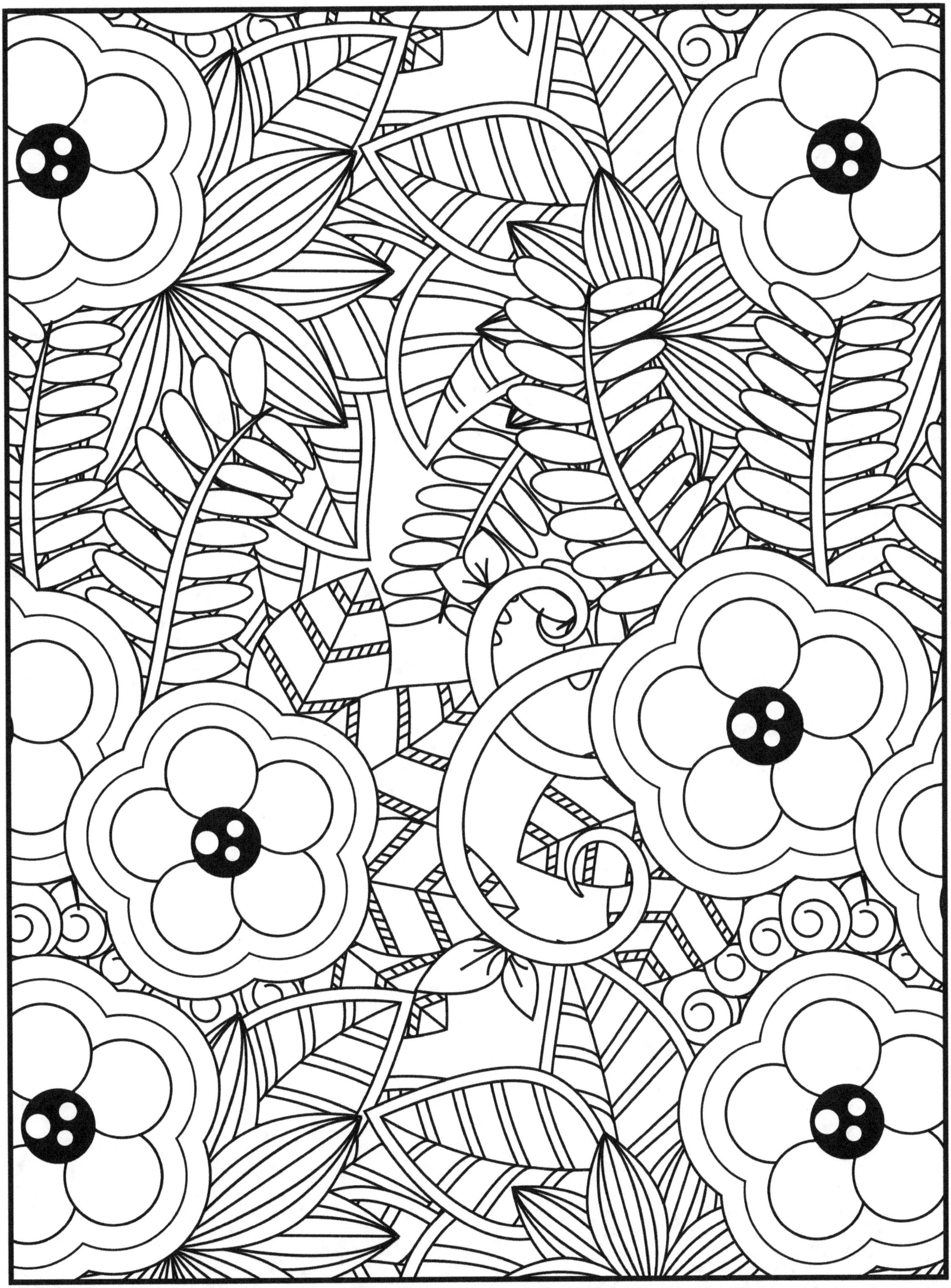

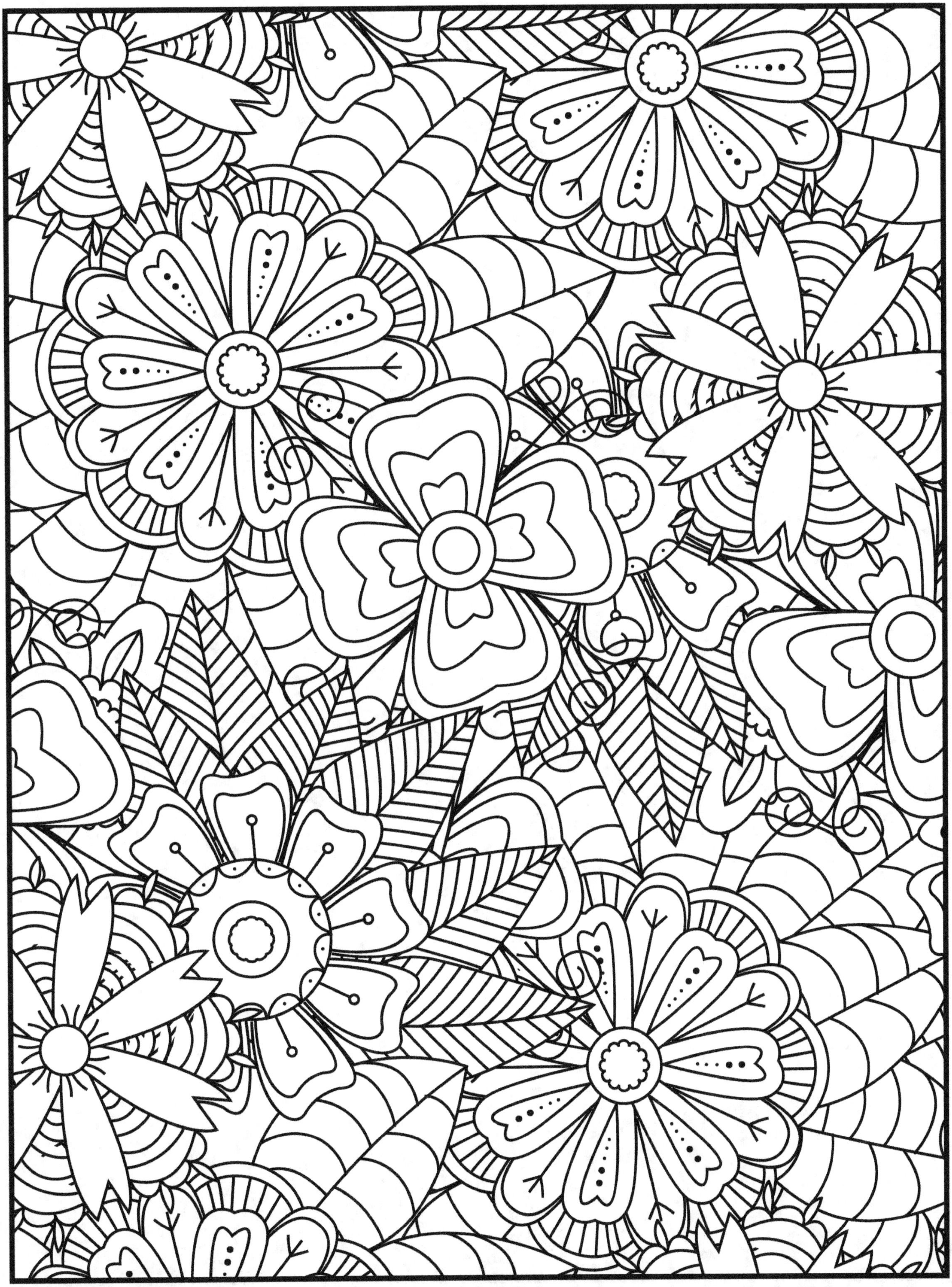

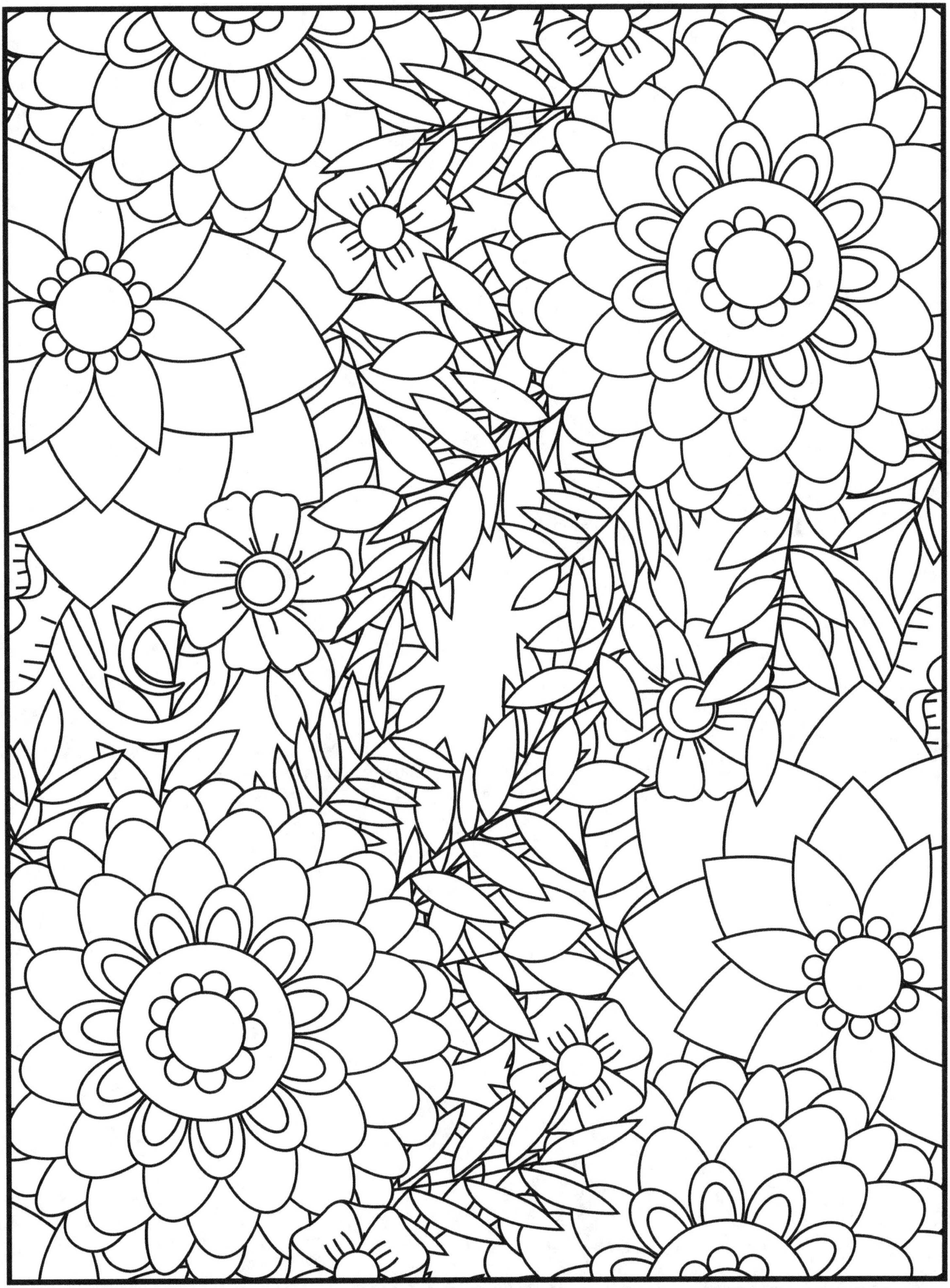

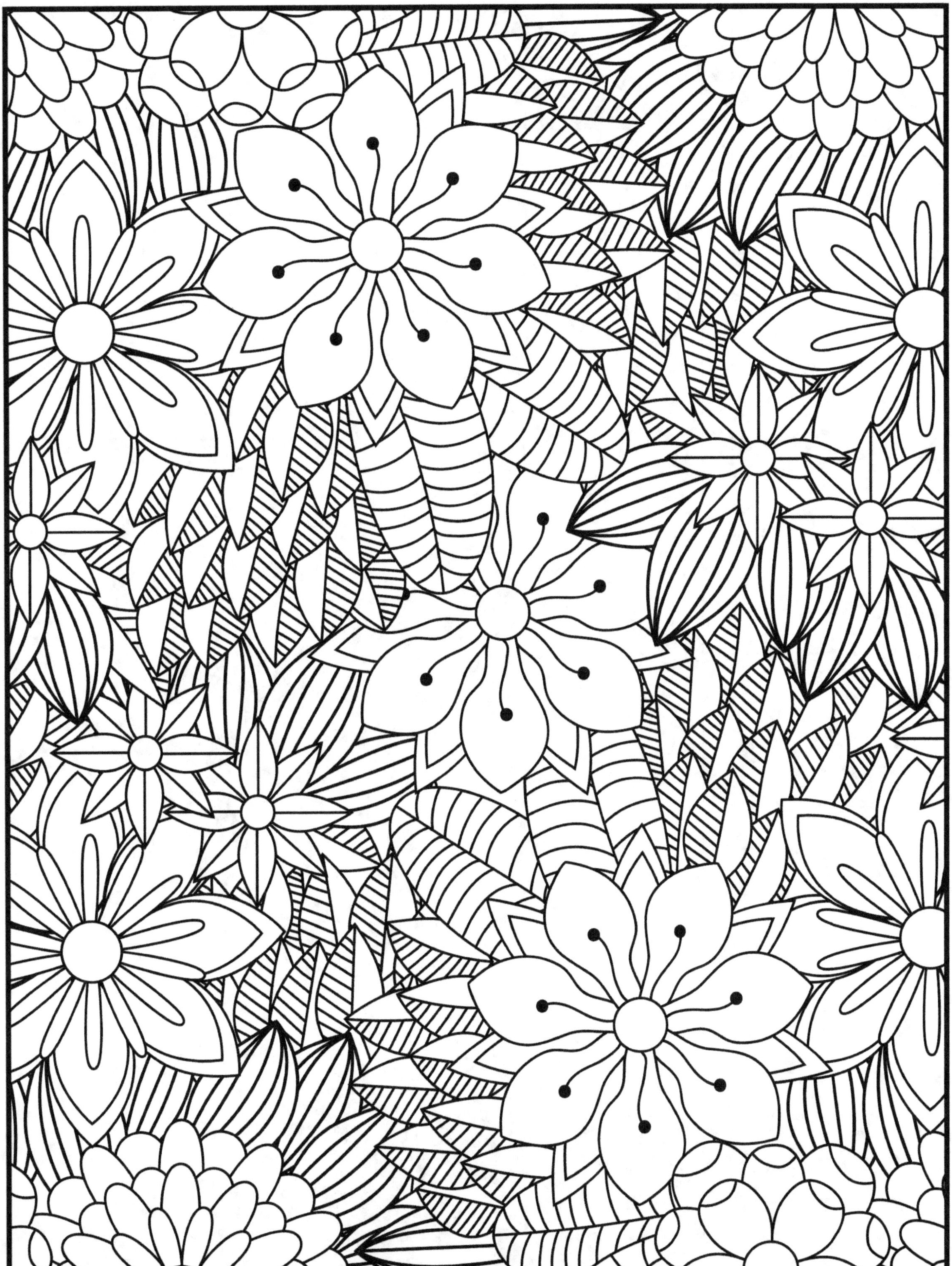

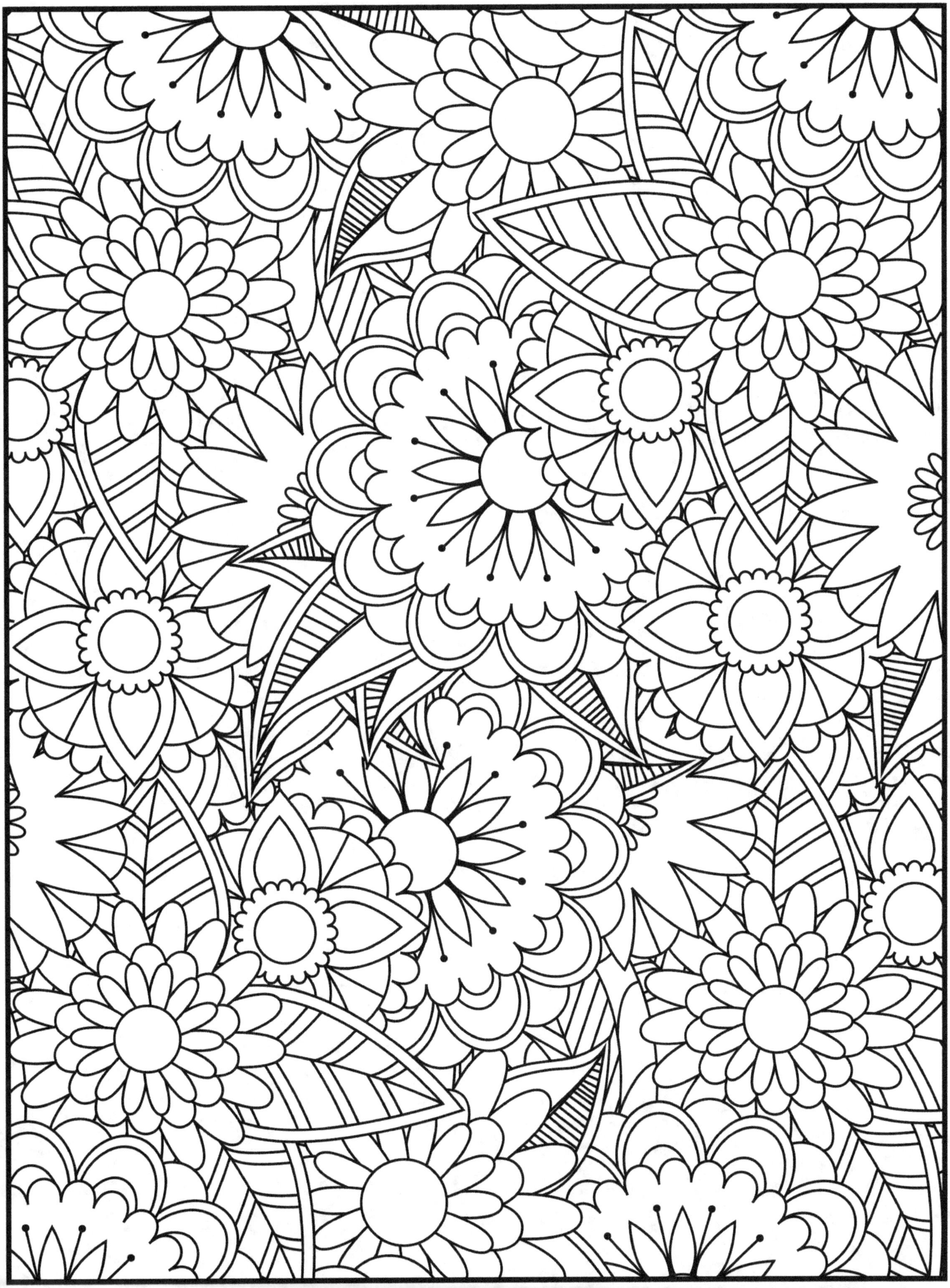

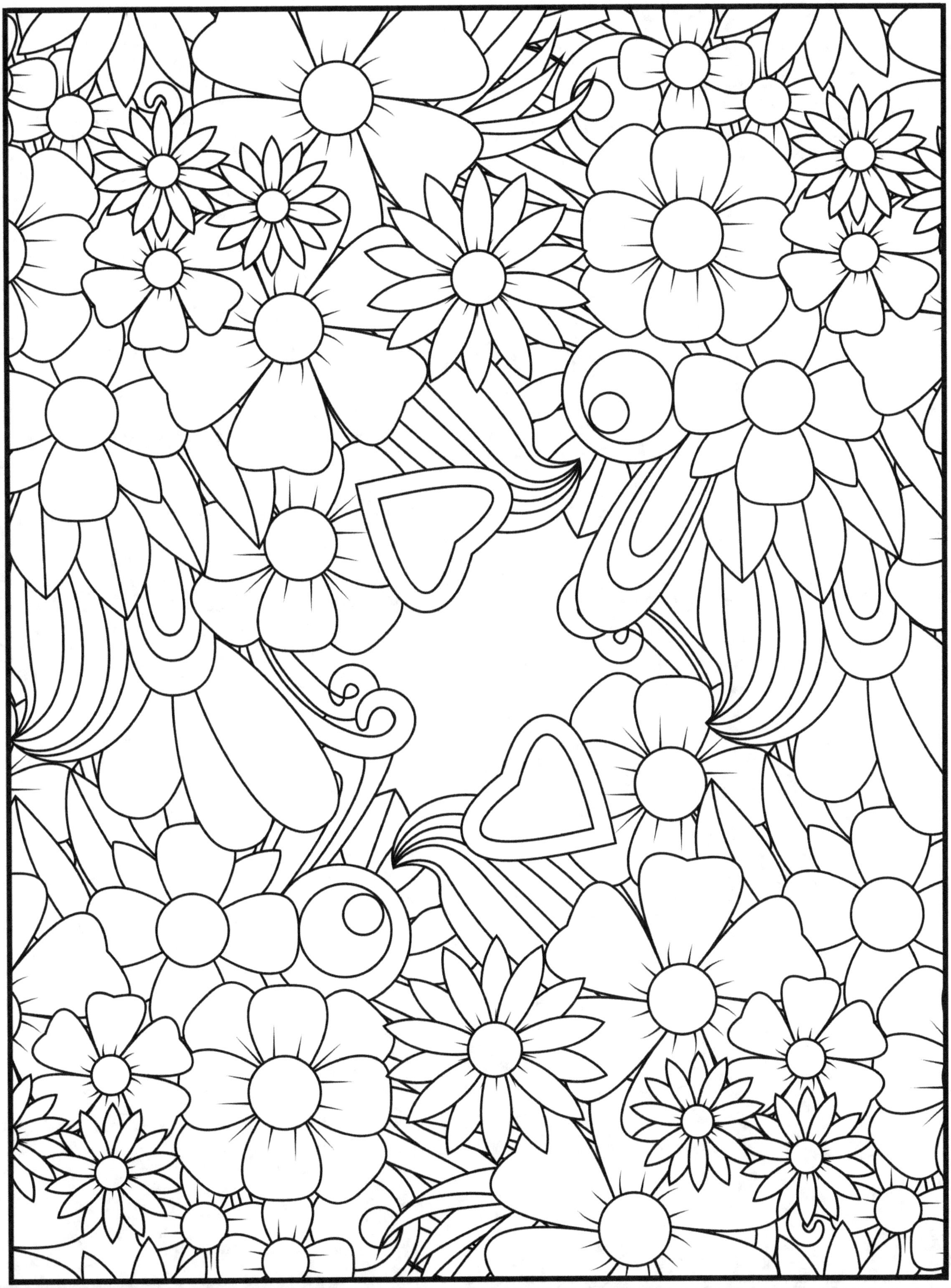

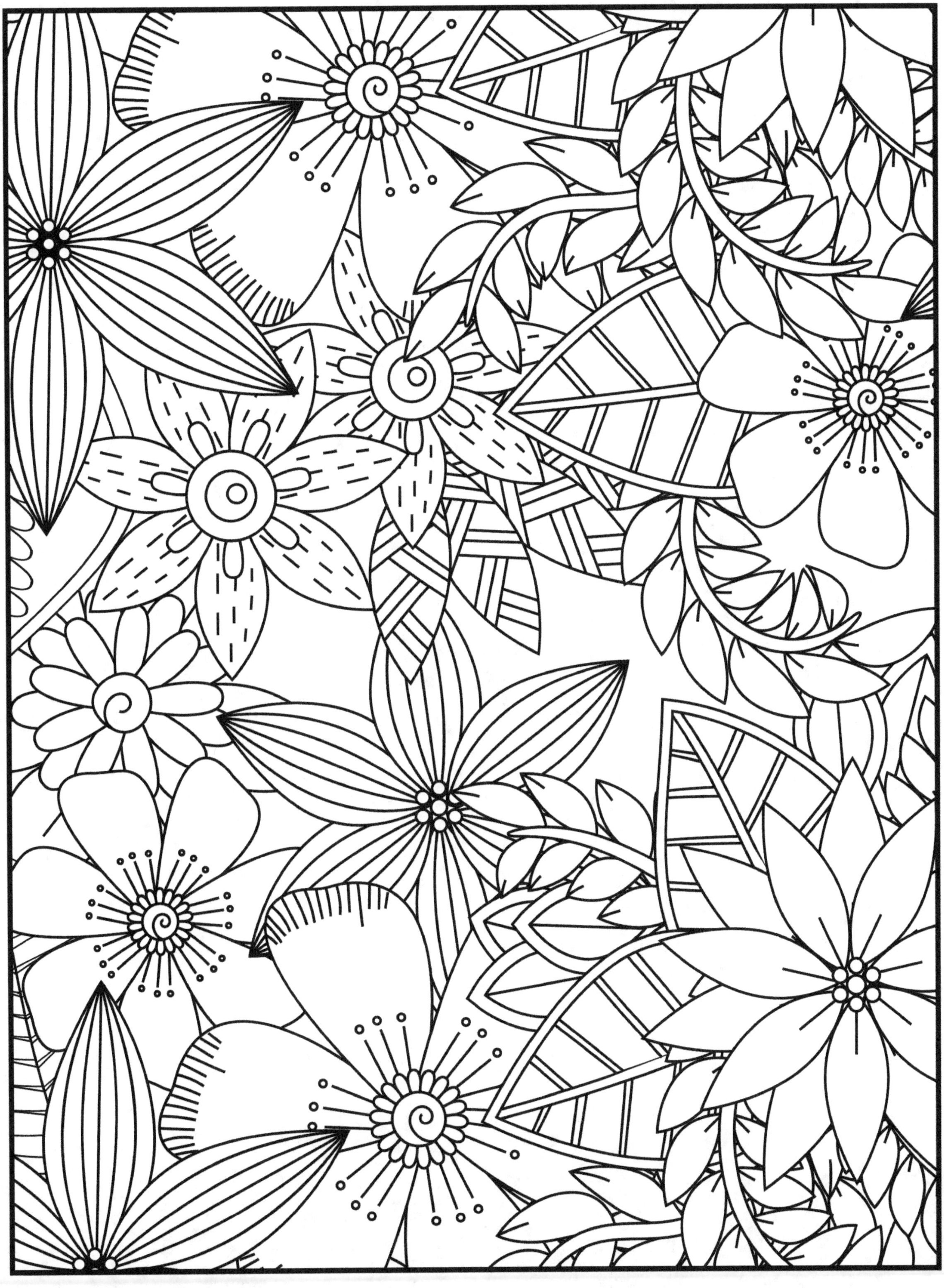

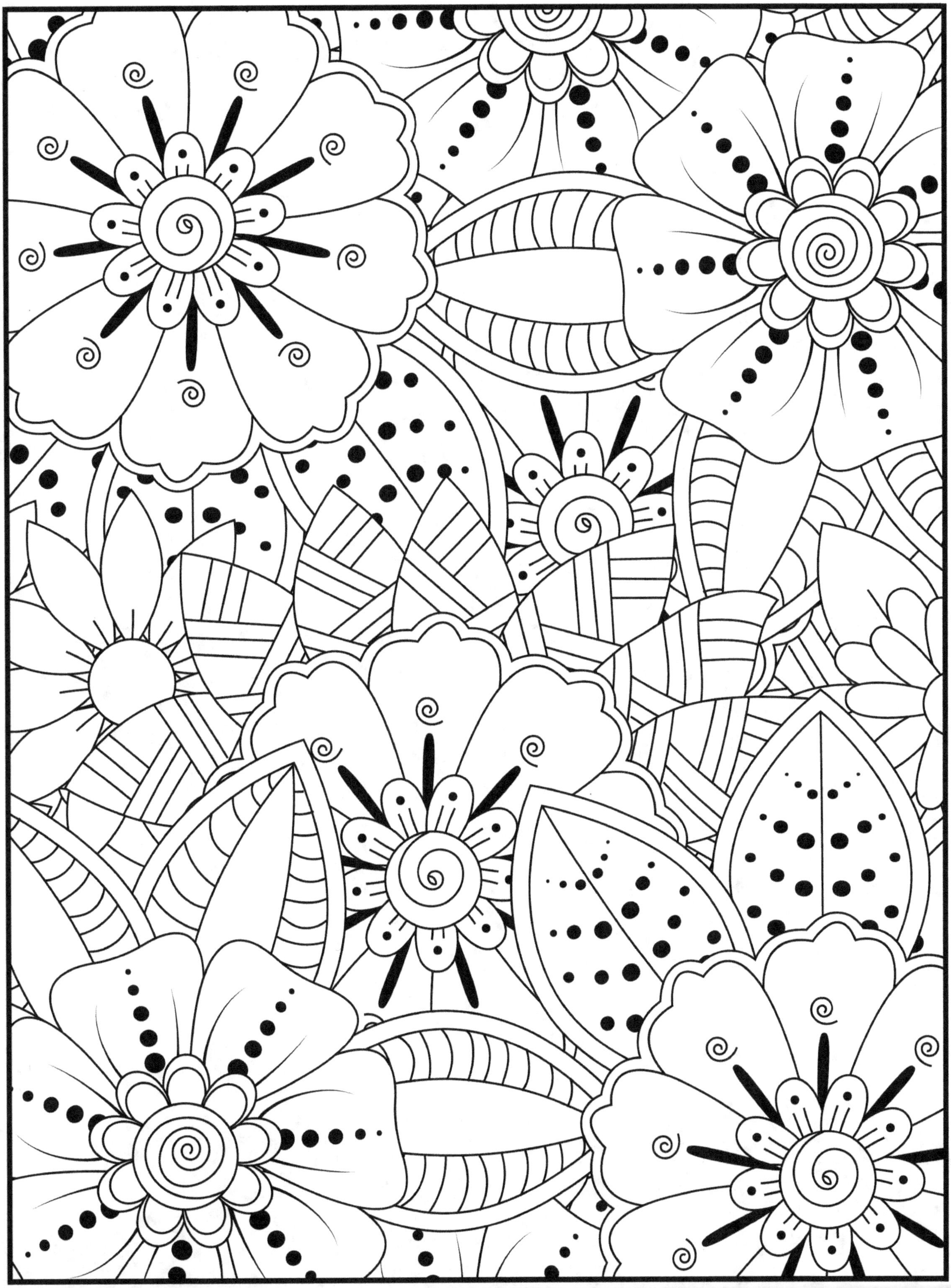

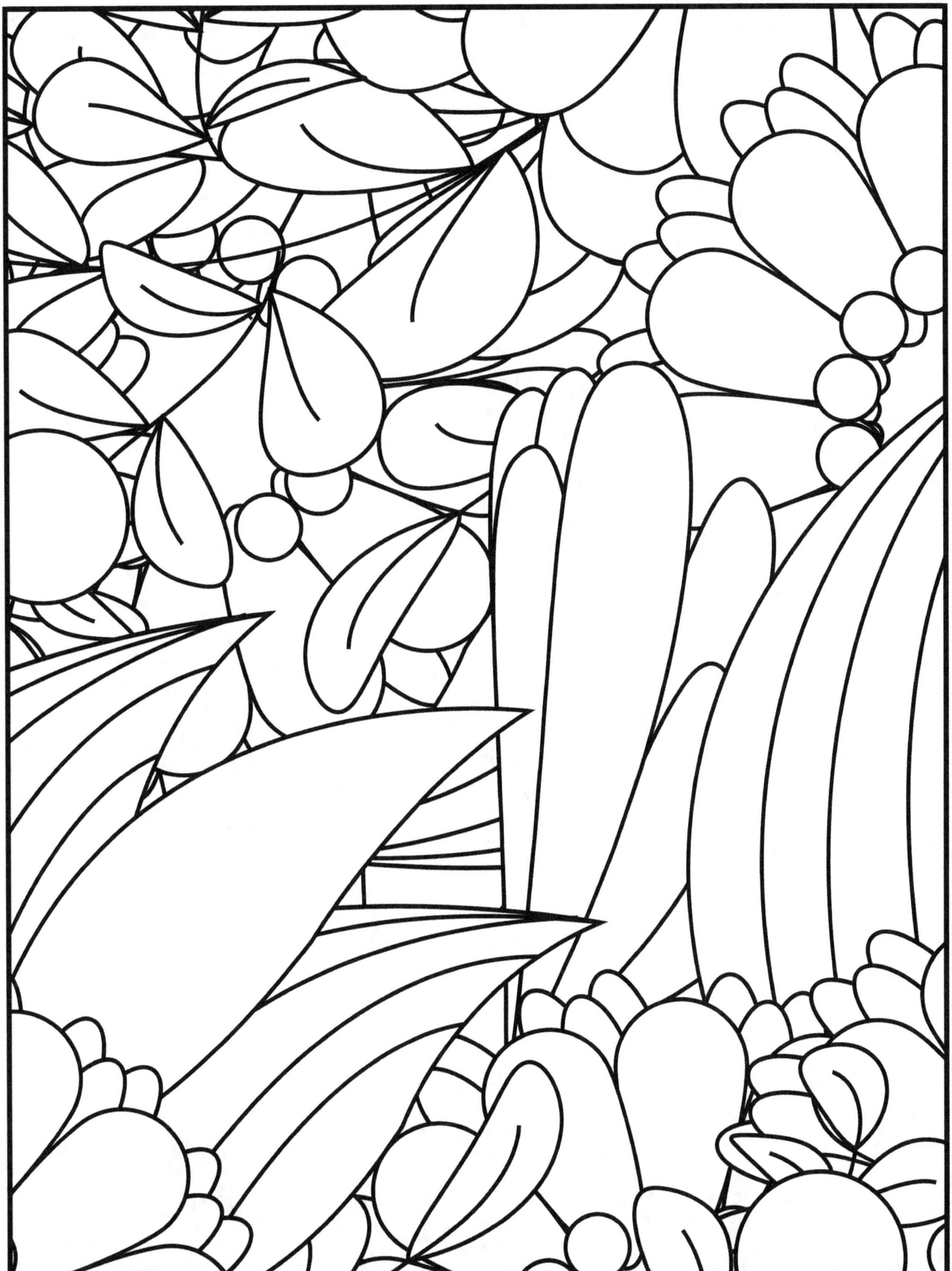

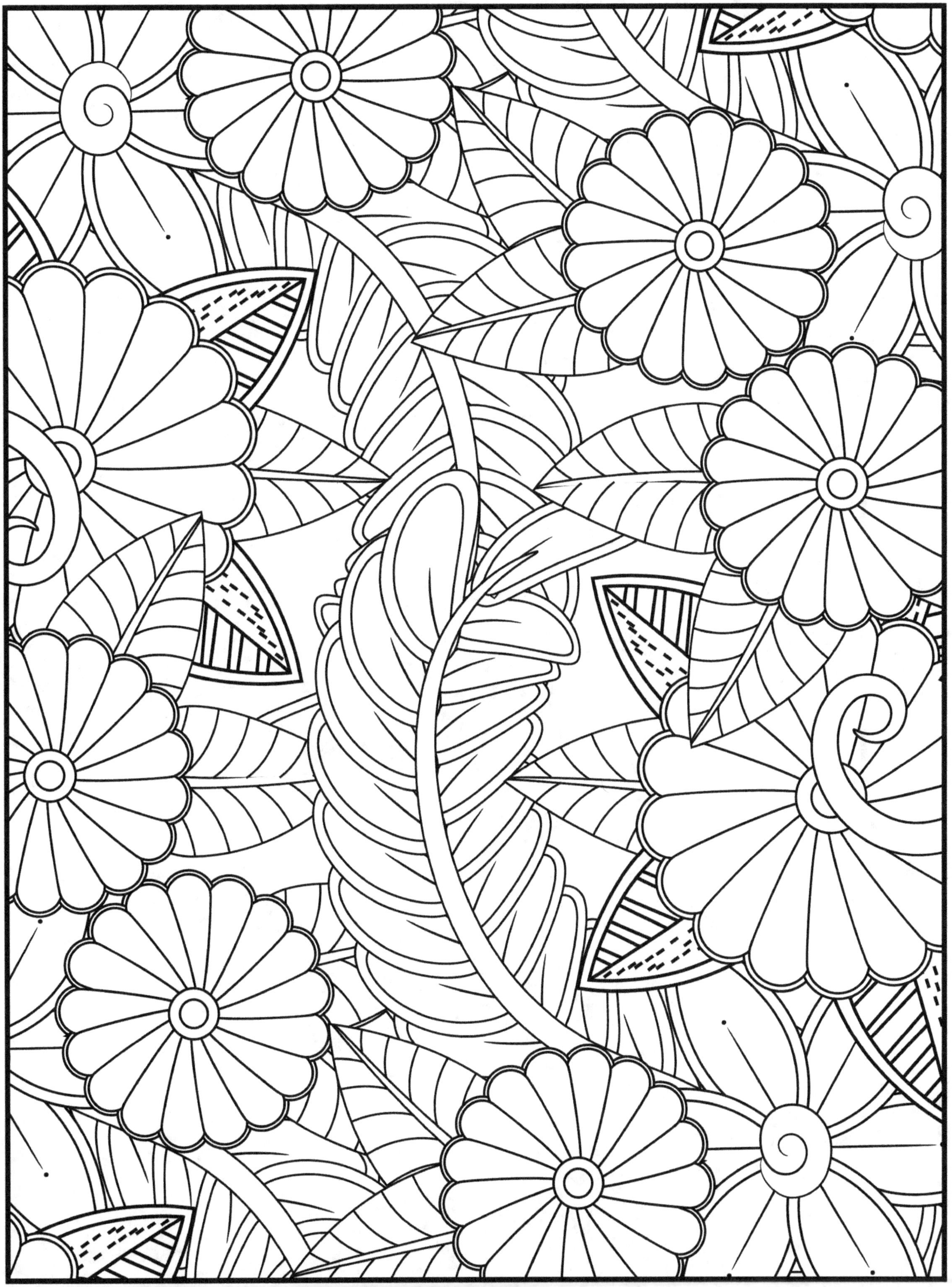

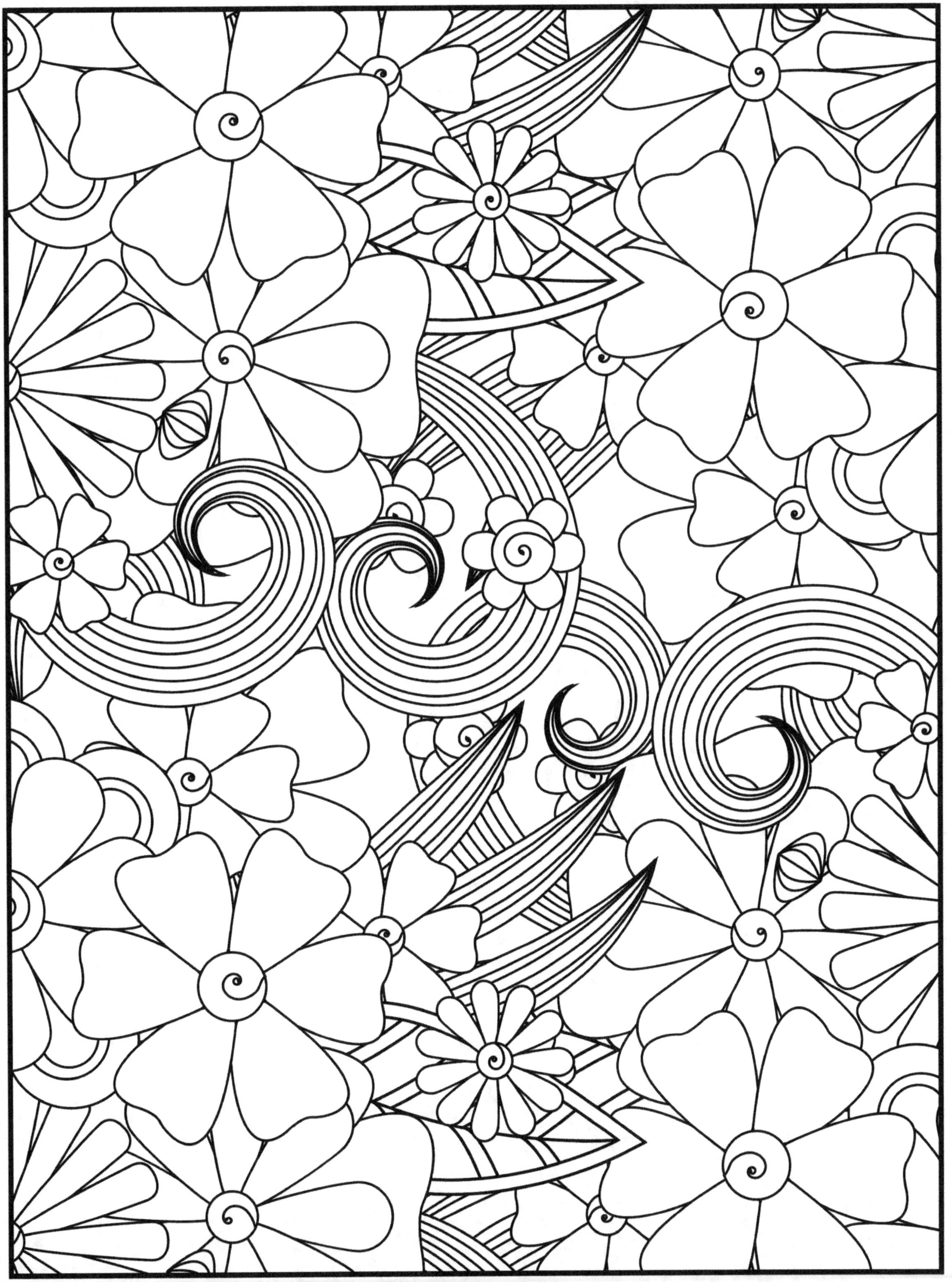

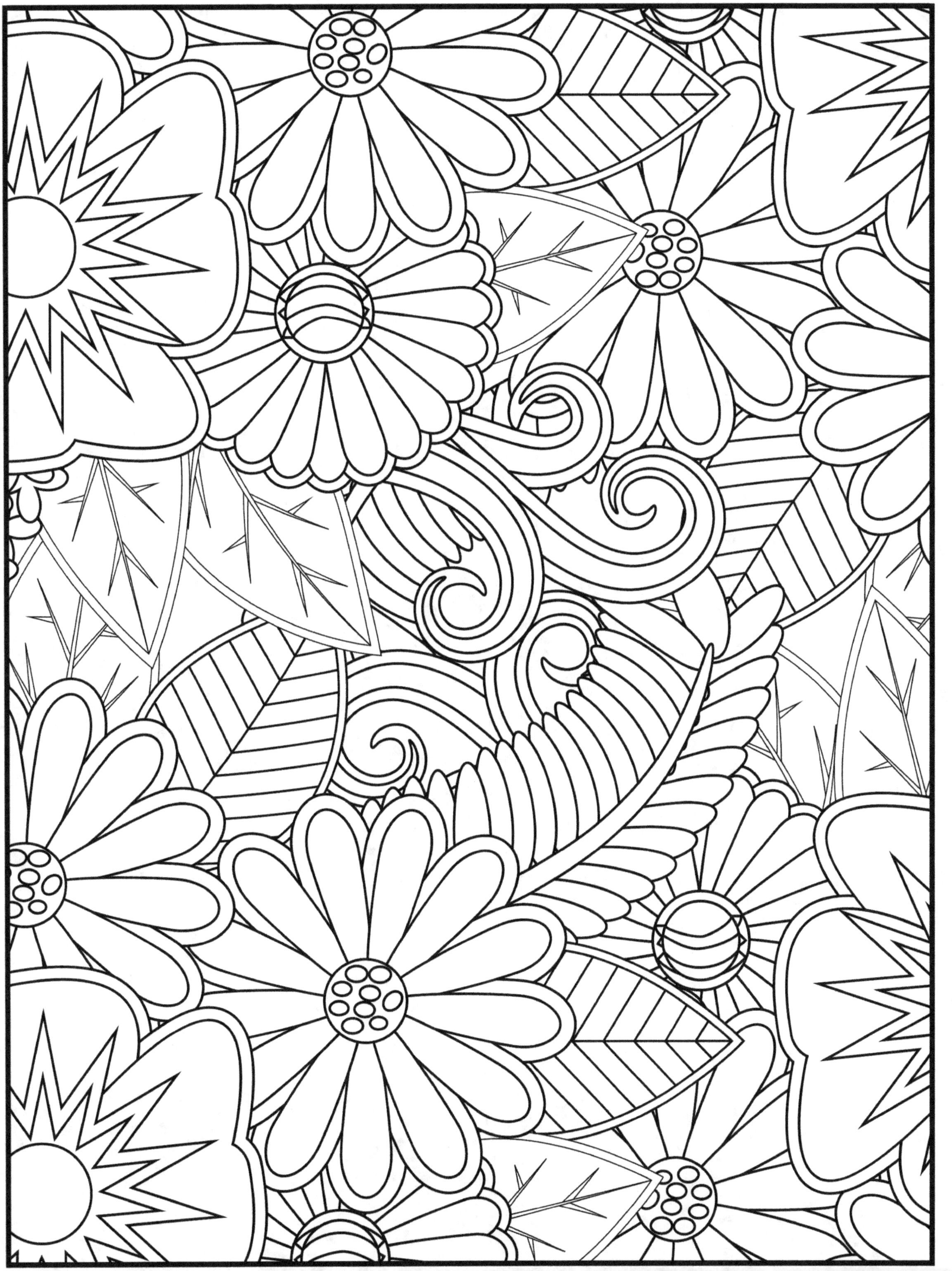

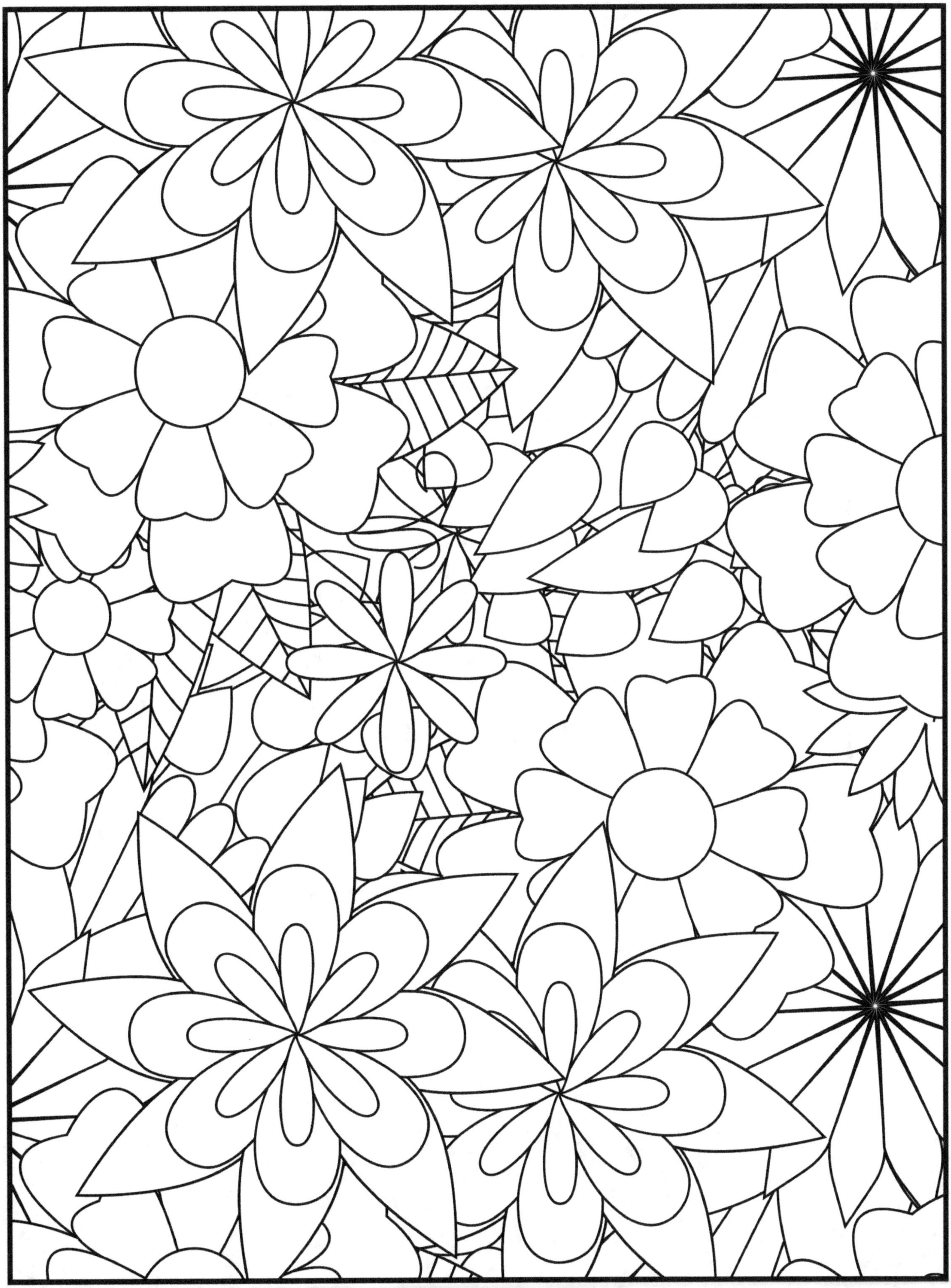

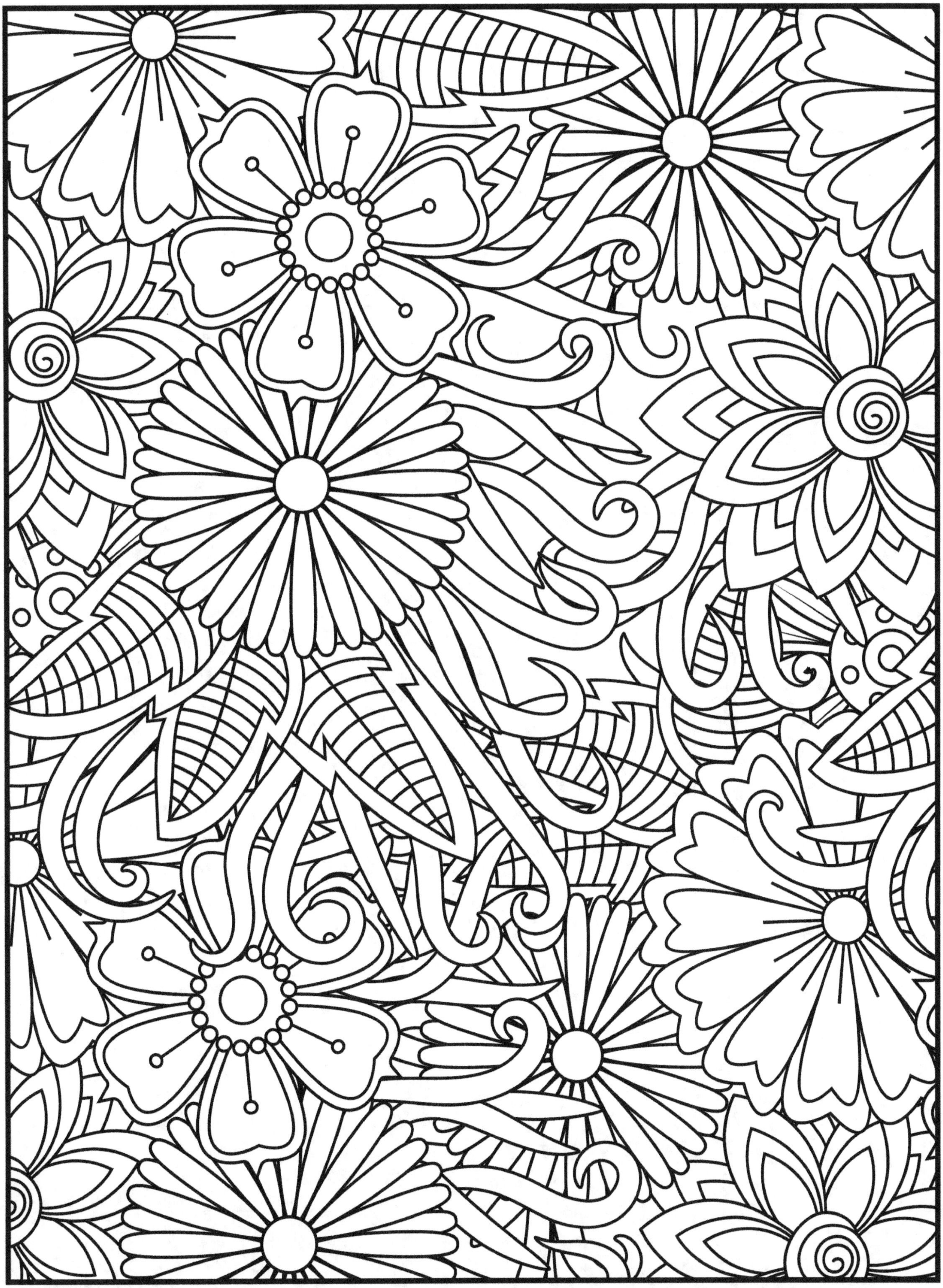

www.ingramcontent.com/pod-product-compliance
Lightning Source LLC
Chambersburg PA
CBHW060422220526
45465CB00008B/2983
9798804609963